Lavenham Church Cookbook

Compiled by
EVELYN CURTIS

Colour artwork and line drawings
by John McLean, Colchester, Essex

First published 1999
Reprinted 2003

Published by

Evelyn Curtis
Sunset House
3 The Glebe
Lavenham, Suffolk CO10 9SN

Designed and printed by
The Lavenham Press, Lavenham, Suffolk CO10 9RN

Introduction

THE idea of Lavenham's Church having its own cookbook to sell on the bookstall came about last year whilst I was doing a bit of research for my monthly cookery article. It occurred to me that although there was a surfeit of glossy cookbooks on the market, and I have plenty of them on my book shelves, it was to the very old tried and tested recipes I turned to when I was stuck for inspiration. Among these were the many cookbooks I have collected from churches I have visited over the years, and I suddenly realised that Lavenham's St. Peter and St. Paul Church did not have a cookbook of its own to sell and raise funds for the church.

Well, I planned to rectify this, and began by first sounding out the idea of a *Lavenham Church Cookbook* on my husband, who manages the bookstall. I was pretty sure he would be in favour of any new venture that would make money for the bookstall and church, and he was, after I had assured him that he wouldn't have to compile it! So that is how it all began.

News soon got around about a possible cookbook, with an amazing response for recipes, and my thanks go to all the contributors to this book which made this project possible, and for their support and good wishes for its success. My thanks also to John McLean, a local artist, who did the excellent line drawings for me. My special thanks go to my long suffering husband and daughter, who have had to sample many of the recipes for me, and managed to survive!

It has been an exciting experience putting this book together, and by buying it I am sure you will enjoy sharing other people's recipes – I know I have! The book itself makes an excellent gift for a relative or friend, and all funds from the sale of it will go towards the upkeep of Lavenham's beautiful church. I am sure too that it will prove to be a great attraction on the bookstall and, who knows, may even become a bestseller!

Evelyn Curtis
Lavenham

3

**This book is dedicated to
all the people in Lavenham
both past and present**

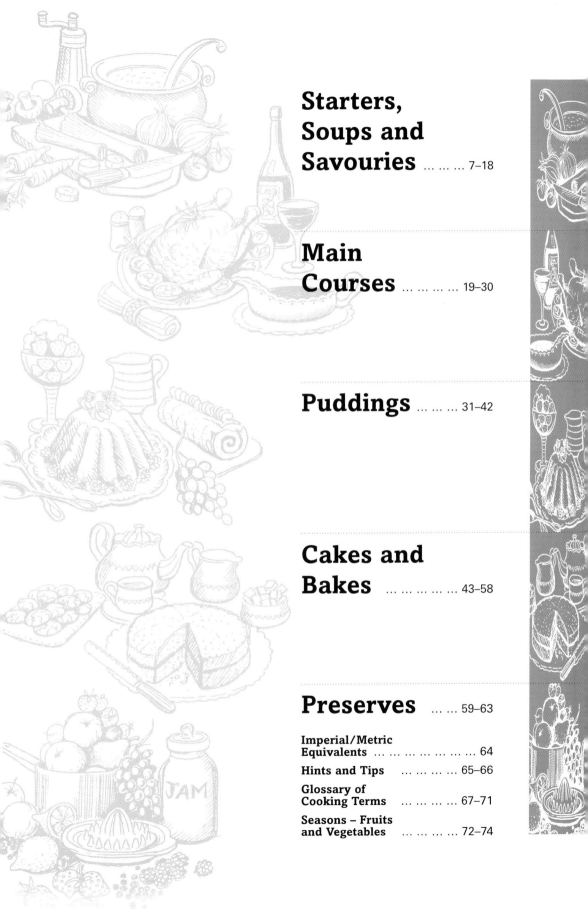

Starters, Soups and Savouries 7–18

Main Courses 19–30

Puddings 31–42

Cakes and Bakes 43–58

Preserves 59–63

Imperial/Metric Equivalents 64

Hints and Tips 65–66

Glossary of Cooking Terms 67–71

Seasons – Fruits and Vegetables 72–74

Starters, Soups and Savouries

Onion and Anchovy Tart 8

Courgette and Pepper Soup 8

Apricot Starter 8

Broccoli and Cheese Soup 9

Salmon Mousse 9

Ham, Cheese and Leek Roll 9

Chilled Pumpkin and
Orange Soup 10

Celery Baked in Cream 10

Cheese Souffle 10

Black Olive and
Avocado Pate 11

Baked Cheesy Potatoes 11

Avocado, Melon and
Tomato Salad 11

Cushions of Cheese Fondue ... 12

Lentil and Tomato Soup 12

Melon Surprise 12

Curried Parsnip and
Orange Soup 13

Niçoise Style Salad with
Parmesan Tuilles 13

Tomato Mousse 14

Tuna Salad Niçoise 14

Mushroom Soup 14

Quick Avocado Starter 15

Calves Liver with Whisky
and Tarragon 15

Curried Egg Mousse 15

Macaroni Cheese with
Broccoli 16

Vegetable Soup 16

Mixed Leaf and Rocket
Salad with Sweet and
Sour Dressing 17

Ratatouille 17

Bortsch (Borsch or Borshch) ... 18

ONION AND ANCHOVY TART

Serves 8

1 x 8 inch shortcrust pastry case
4 large onions, finely sliced
1 tin of anchovies
150 ml (¼ pt) double cream
2 eggs
Salt and pepper to taste
115 g (4 oz) butter

Put a heavy based pan on the stove, melt the butter and gently fry the onions until soft and caramelised. Remove from the heat and let the onions cool. Stir in the eggs, cream, salt and pepper and place the mixture in the flan case.

Decorate with the anchovies and bake in the oven at 180°C, 350°F, Gas Mark 4, until the mixture is firm to the touch. Serve warm.

Roy and Anne Whitworth
John and Val Barry
The Angel
Lavenham
Suffolk

COURGETTE AND PEPPER SOUP

Appeals to the eye as well as the palate!
Serves 4–6

450 g (1 lb) courgettes, grated
1 red and 1 green pepper, finely diced
1 x 400 g tin chopped tomatoes
4 sticks of celery, chopped
1 small onion, chopped
2 cloves garlic, peeled
25 g (1 oz) butter
1.2 ltrs (2 pts) vegetable stock
6–8 basil leaves, or 1 tsp dried basil
Seasoning

In a large pan, sweat off the celery, onion and garlic in the butter. Add half of the vegetable stock and bring to the boil, simmer for 5 minutes then add the tomatoes and basil. Allow to cool, then liquidise until smooth.

Pour back into the pan, add the remaining stock, the courgettes and peppers, season well and bring back to just below boiling point (at this stage 1 tbsp of cornflour could be added if a thick soup is preferred), simmer for 5–10 minutes. *Do not boil.* Freezes well.

The Bishop of St. Edmundsbury
and Ipswich, The Right Reverend
Richard Lewis

APRICOT STARTER

On a lettuce leaf lay half cooked apricots, 2–3 for each person according to size. Roast some blanched almonds, chop and mix with cream cheese.

Fill the centres of the apricots and sprinkle with chopped parsley. Very decorative and tasty!
Evelyn Curtis
Lavenham

BROCCOLI AND CHEESE SOUP

Serves approximately 6

1 medium onion, peeled
175 g (6 oz) potatoes, peeled
1 tbsp sunflower oil
450 g (1 lb) broccoli
Salt and pepper
½ tsp sugar
1.2 ltrs (2 pts) water or chicken stock
175 g (6 oz) mature Cheddar
   cheese, grated not less than
   strength 4 (for the more
   adventurous try English Stilton)

Chop the onion and potatoes roughly and fry gently in the oil. Trim the broccoli and cut the stems into ½ inch slices. Add the stems to the potato and onion mixture. Fry for 5 minutes and season generously.

Reserve half the broccoli florets and add to the potato mixture, adding the water (or chicken stock if you prefer a richer soup). Simmer for 20 minutes until the vegetables are soft. Add the remaining florets and the sugar, cook for 1 minute and put into a food processor or liquidiser and blend. Most of the soup will become smooth, but the newly added broccoli will retain a slight grainy texture.

Pour into a soup tureen or large casserole and sprinkle on the grated cheese, stirring and turning with a ladle for a minute or two until the cheese is melted in the soup. Serve with wholemeal or rye bread or crusty brown rolls.

Maureen Allen
Lavenham

SALMON MOUSSE

230 g (8 oz) cooked salmon
115 g (4 oz) smoked salmon
230 g (8 oz) cream cheese
Juice of half a lemon
2 tbsp mayonnaise
Pinch of paprika
30 g (1 oz) fresh white
   breadcrumbs
2 tbsp whipped cream
Salt and pepper to taste

Blend salmon in a food processor to a puree. Add all the other ingredients and blend together. Turn into a mould and leave in the fridge until set.

Roy and Anne Whitworth
John and Val Barry
The Angel
Lavenham
Suffolk

HAM, CHEESE AND LEEK ROLL

Makes a very tasty supper dish, or a light lunch,
served with granary bread and a glass of white wine!

Take the required number of medium sized leeks. Cheese – mature Cheddar (or of your choice). Ham.

Take the leeks and boil until cooked, but still firm. Roll in fresh cooked ham, not too thin. Grate the cheese over the ham rolls and grill until cheese has melted.

Doreen Brinkley
Lavenham

CHILLED PUMPKIN AND ORANGE SOUP

Serves 6

450 g (1 lb) pumpkin, peeled and
    roughly chopped
115 g (4 oz) onions, roughly chopped
1 sprig of thyme and 1 bayleaf
6 oranges
1 tbsp picked coriander
1.2 ltrs (2½ pts) vegetable stock
60 g (2 oz) sugar
60 g (2 oz) butter
60 g (2 oz) flour

Sweat onions, pumpkin, thyme and bayleaf in a pan in the butter. Add flour and cook out, then add the vegetable stock. Bring to the boil and then simmer for an hour. In a separate pan, juice the oranges and add the sugar. Reduce to a syrup. When the soup has finished cooking add the orange reduction, then blend, pass and chill. To serve place soup in a shallow bowl and sprinkle with roughly chopped coriander.

Alan Ford, Head Chef
Hintlesham Hall
Hintlesham, Suffolk

CELERY BAKED IN CREAM

1 large head of celery
¼ tsp ground allspice
300 ml (½ pt) single cream
Salt and pepper
30 g (1 oz) fresh wholemeal
    breadcrumbs

Reserve a few celery leaves to garnish, then cut sticks lengthways into thin strips. Cut each strip into 2 inch lengths and put into an oven-proof serving dish. Mix allspice and cream together and season to taste. Pour over the celery, sprinkle with breadcrumbs.

Bake at 200°C, 400°F, Gas Mark 6, until celery is tender. Serve hot garnished with reserved celery leaves.

Rosemary Wheeler
Cambridge

CHEESE SOUFFLE

Beat 2 eggs in a little less than 300 ml (½ pt) milk. Add 170 g (6 oz) grated cheese, 1 small onion, finely chopped, 1 tbsp mayonnaise, a little thyme, or, other herbs, a suggestion of garlic powder and a pinch of nutmeg and a small knob of butter. Turn into a greased oven-proof dish and bake for half to three quarters of an hour at 190°C, 375°F, Gas Mark 5, until golden brown and set.

Eileen Huffey, Lavenham

■ I have tried this recipe and it is delicious. Can be used for a light lunch or supper dish, or alternatively, fill small ramekin dishes garnish with parsley, and serve as a starter for 4.

Evelyn Curtis

BLACK OLIVE
AND AVOCADO PATE

Serves 4

1 medium can black olives
2 ripe avocados
2 tbsp olive oil
2 cloves garlic
175 g (6 oz) breadcrumbs
Black pepper to taste

Blend olives and avocados in food processor. Add garlic, olive oil and pepper. Then add breadcrumbs to the mixture, to make it all come together (the breadcrumbs help to increase the bulk).

Put into a dish or individual ramekins. Does not need cooking.

John Carr
Lavenham

BAKED CHEESY POTATOES

I first tried this recipe at school, at the age of 12 –
always a favourite at home!

Large potatoes (one for each person)
60–85 g (2–3 oz) Cheddar cheese,
   grated
Butter or margarine

Bake the potatoes until soft and ready to take out of their skins.

Mash the potato until soft and creamy – add a little milk. Add some butter or margarine and then add the grated cheese and mix in. Once everything is mixed in put back into the potato skins.

Sprinkle some grated cheese onto the potatoes before putting under the grill. Add sprigs of parsley to garnish.

Belinda Curtis
Lavenham

AVOCADO, MELON
AND TOMATO SALAD

6 tomatoes
2 avocados
1 tbsp lemon juice
1 small melon
6 tbsp French dressing
Mint leaves

Skin tomatoes, cut in half and scrape out seeds. Cut into wedges. Skin the avocados, remove stones and cut flesh into chunks. Sprinkle with lemon juice. Cut melon flesh into chunks. Mix all together in a glass bowl with chopped mint leaves.

Pour on dressing 30 minutes before serving.

Jane Bean
Lavenham

CUSHIONS OF CHEESE FONDUE

Can be prepared up to two days in advance.

Bechamel:
100 g (3½ oz) butter
100 g (3½ oz) plain flour
600 ml (1 pt) milk
300 g (10½ oz) grated Cheddar
300 g (10½ oz) grated Gruyere
Salt, pepper, 150 ml (about ¼ pt)
white wine, 150 ml (about ¼ pt)
whipping cream, 1 capful Kirsch
To garnish: *Breadcrumbs, egg, flour*

Prepare the Bechamel with butter, flour and milk. Add grated Cheddar/Gruyere, small amounts at a time, on a low flame. Add white wine, Kirsch, cream, seasoning. Pour into a baking dish and leave it to cool and set in the fridge. Cut into 3 cm cubes (about 1 inch), roll them in egg, flour and breadcrumbs. Fry them until golden in very hot oil. The centre must be melting.

Serve with garlic mayonnaise and salad.

Signature dish: Regis Crepy's
Cushions of Cheese Fondue
The Great House
Lavenham

LENTIL AND TOMATO SOUP

Serve with grated cheese and croutons. Satisfying soup.
Sometimes I use a tin of chopped tomatoes if I am in a hurry.

1 small onion
230 g (8 oz) tomatoes
2 tbsp oil
115 g (4 oz) lentils (split orange)
300 ml (½ pt) tomato juice
850 ml (1½ pts) vegetable or
chicken stock (or stock cube)
½ tsp thyme
½ tsp marmite
Salt and pepper

Chop the onion and tomatoes. Heat oil in saucepan and saute the onion until transparent. Add remaining ingredients, cover and simmer for 30 minutes. Adjust seasoning to taste.

Serve as is, or "blend" it, which is what I do.

Barbara Pearmain
Lavenham

MELON SURPRISE

Ogen melons (adjust to number
of servings)
Brandy (or sherry) and champagne
Maraschina cherries
Ginger in syrup

Cut the melons in halves and remove seeds. Place cherries in the centre with the ginger and add some ginger syrup.

Add the brandy (or sherry) and champagne and serve.

Doreen Brinkley
Lavenham

CURRIED PARSNIP AND ORANGE SOUP

Serves 4–6

60 g (2 oz) butter
2 parsnips, peeled and diced
1 onion, skinned and chopped
1 garlic clove, skinned and crushed
1 tsp curry powder
1 tsp ground cumin
1 tbsp flour
1.4 ltrs (2 pts) chicken stock
Rind and juice of 2 large oranges
Salt and pepper

Melt butter in a large saucepan. Add parsnips and onion, cover the pan and fry gently for 10 minutes until softened, shaking the pan frequently.

Add the garlic and spice and fry uncovered for 2 minutes. Stir in the flour, cook for a further 2 minutes then pour in the stock and orange juice. Bring to the boil. Season. Simmer for about 20 minutes until parsnips are tender. Turn into a blender or food processor and blend.

Margaret Morley
Lavenham

NIÇOISE STYLE SALAD WITH PARMESAN TUILLES

Seasonal leaves
230 g (8 oz) French beans, topped, tailed and cooked
3 tomatoes, blanched and skinned
15 quails eggs, boiled for 5 minutes
6 anchovy fillets, cut into fine strips (optional)
60 g (2 oz) black olives, stoned and cut in half
30 g (1 oz) capers
1 tsp lemon juice
Basil leaves
Olive oil
60 g (2 oz) fresh Parmesan, finely grated, pinch of Cheddar cheese
Seasoning

Sprinkle grated Parmesan onto baking tray to form 2 inch circles. Cook in a hot oven until light brown, remove from oven and allow to cool slightly, then remove from baking tray and mould over a rolling pin.

Cut the tomatoes into half, deseed, then cut into 3. Peel the quails eggs and cut in half. Season beans and toss with olive oil and arrange on plates.

Scatter tomato petals around plate, then position 5 x ½ quails eggs around, sprinkle capers and olives around.

Pick some basil leaves and mix with the salad leaves and place a small pile in the centre of the plate.

Chop 1 tbsp of basil and mix with 4 tbsp of olive oil and 1 tsp of lemon juice, pour around, scatter (anchovy fillets over salad, if used), and 3 tuilles around salad.

Alan Ford, Head Chef
Hintlesham Hall
Hintlesham
Suffolk

TOMATO MOUSSE

A nice starter for a summer's day.
Serves 6

600 ml (1 pt) tomato juice, less
  2 tbsp
2 tbsp boiling water
1 sachet powered gelatine
1 dsp lemon juice
½ tsp Worcester sauce
1 tsp caster sugar
Salt and pepper
1 cup diced vegetables – eg
  cucumber, peas, pepper, tomato
  (optional)

Dissolve gelatine in water, stir in tomato juice, add other ingredients and mix well.

Pour into individual glass moulds or ramekin dishes. Leave to set in fridge.

Decorate with parsley, black olives, prawns or chopped egg, as you wish.

Evelyn Curtis
Lavenham

TUNA SALAD NIÇOISE

50 g (1¾ oz) haricot vert, picked
  and cooked al dente
15 g (½ oz) red onions, finely
  sliced
Balsamic dressing
1 pomme nouvelle, boiled, peeled
  and sliced
3½ small cherry tomatoes
3½ soft boiled quail eggs
60 g (2 oz) tuna steak, cooked pink
Salt and pepper

Season the haricot vert salad and onions with salt, pepper and balsamic vinegar. Place the mixture into a medium sized grey ring and press down so it is level. Arrange the sliced potato on top and place the ring onto the centre of the plate. Dribble some of the dressing around the plate and arrange the tomatoes and eggs around the plate. Remove the ring then cut the tuna in half at an angle and place on top of the salad.

Anton Edelmann
Maître Chef des Cuisines
The Savoy
London WC2

MUSHROOM SOUP

910 g (2 lb) mushrooms
230 g (8 oz) butter
2 large onions
115 g (4 oz) flour
1.4 ltrs (2 pts) water
1.4 ltrs (2 pts) milk
Salt and pepper to taste

Place mushrooms, butter, onions and water into a large saucepan, bring to boil and simmer until mushrooms and onions are soft. Liquidise and return to saucepan. Add flour to the milk and stir. Add to saucepan and bring to the boil. Add salt and pepper to taste.

Cindy King
Chilcompton
Somerset

QUICK AVOCADO STARTER

Serves 4

2 avocado pears
Lemon juice
Black pepper
2 tbsp double cream
2 egg whites
Watercress to garnish

Skin, stone and mash the avocados. Add about 1 tsp lemon juice, black pepper and mix well.

Beat the cream and add to mixture. Whip the egg whites and combine with the avocado and cream. Serve in individual dishes and garnish with watercress.

**From the cookery book of
the Voluntary Research Trust of
King's College Hospital and
Medical School**

CALVES LIVER WITH WHISKY AND TARRAGON

Serves 4

4 thin slices of calves liver
150 ml (¼ pt) chicken stock
Fresh tarragon leaves thinly
   chopped
1 measure of whisky
Salt, pepper and sugar

Coat calves liver in seasoned flour. Heat a large frying pan with enough oil to cover the bottom. Add liver and cook for 2 minutes on each side. Remove from pan and keep warm. Drain any excess oil from the

pan. Add chicken stock to the pan and reduce by a third, scraping up any burnt bits into the stock. Add whisky and tarragon plus a pinch of sugar and simmer gently for 2 minutes. Adjust seasoning and then pour over the liver garnishing with a few extra tarragon leaves.

**Roy and Anne Whitworth
John and Val Barry
The Angel, Lavenham
Suffolk**

CURRIED EGG MOUSSE

Serves 8

7 hard boiled eggs, chopped
230 ml (8 fl oz) aspic jelly (or
   chicken stock with gelatine)
2 tbsp curry paste
300 ml (½ pt) mayonnaise
Dash of Worcester sauce
Few drops of tabasco sauce
Fresh herbs
200 ml (⅓ pt) whipped cream
Extra 300 ml (½ pt) aspic jelly (or
   similar)

Mix all together, except cream and extra aspic jelly. Season well. Chill until starting to set. Fold in whipped cream and put into serving dish. When set, put extra aspic on top with pieces of herbs to decorate. Leave in fridge to set (2–3 hours). Serve with toast or biscuits.

**The Duchess of Devonshire
Chatsworth, Bakewell, Derby**

MACARONI CHEESE WITH BROCCOLI

85 g (3 oz) wholewheat macaroni
Salt and pepper
30 g (1 oz) butter
30 g (1 oz) plain flour
300 ml (½ pt) fresh milk
85 g (3 oz) Red Leicester cheese,
   grated
115 g (4 oz) broccoli florets
1 tbsp fresh wholemeal
   breadcrumbs

Cook macaroni in 1.2 ltrs (2 pts) boiling water (salted) for 15 minutes. Drain. Pour butter, flour and milk into saucepan. Heat and whisk continuously until the sauce thickens and is smooth. Simmer for 1–2 minutes. Remove pan from heat, add most of the cheese and stir until melted. Season to taste. Blanch broccoli in boiling water for 7 minutes or until tender. Drain well.

Put broccoli into the base of a 850 ml (1½ pt) flameproof serving dish. Cover with macaroni and cheese sauce. Sprinkle with remaining cheese and breadcrumbs and brown under a hot grill.

Rosemary Wheeler
Cambridge

VEGETABLE SOUP

60 g (2 oz) margarine
4 potatoes, cut into quarters
1 leek, sliced
1 large carrot, grated
1 chicken stock cube, dissolved in
   425 ml (¾ pt) hot water, or fresh
   chicken stock
1 tbsp oatmeal
300 ml (½ pt) milk
Parsley, chopped
Grated cheese (optional)

Melt margarine, add vegetables and stir for a few minutes. Add water and stock cube, or chicken stock, bring to the boil and simmer for half an hour. Mash down the vegetables with potato masher (do not liquidise). Mix oatmeal into milk, add to pan, bring to the boil and simmer for quarter of an hour. When ready, add parsley and cheese (if liked).

Jean Boyd
Lavenham

■ *This recipe was given out on the BBC Radio during the War by the Ministry of Food. It required no meat and as most people then grew potatoes, leeks, etc, in their gardens or allotments, it was easy to make, and adding the oatmeal, milk and cheese made it both filling and nutritious.*

In those days it was often just made with water, as chicken stock was not always readily available, and stock cubes were not around then.

MIXED LEAF AND ROCKET SALAD WITH SWEET AND SOUR DRESSING

Serves 6

60 g (2 oz) rocket leaves
179 g (6 oz) mixed salad leaves

Dressing
¼ tsp garlic, chopped
¼ tsp ginger, chopped
1 shallot, finely chopped
1 tsp red pepper, chopped
1 tsp tomato puree
1 tbsp cucumber, finely diced
1 tbsp brown sugar
3 tbsp balsamic vinegar
6 tbsp olive oil
1 tsp lemon juice

To make the dressing sweat the garlic, ginger, shallots and red pepper in a small amount of olive oil, add the tomato puree and brown sugar and cook for 1 minute. Add 2 tbsp balsamic vinegar and reduce by half, add the diced cucumber and olive oil and cook for a further minute. Remove from heat and add the remaining balsamic vinegar and lemon juice, season and allow cool. Mix the seasonal salad leaves and rocket together, place in the centre of the plate and drizzle the dressing over and around the leaves.

Alan Ford, Head Chef
Hintlesham Hall
Hintlesham, Suffolk

RATATOUILLE

400 g (14 oz) aubergines
400 g (14 oz) courgettes
200 g (7 oz) green pepper
200 ml (7 fl oz) olive oil
200 g (7 oz) onions, diced
1 bouquet garni and herbes de
   Provence
½ garlic bulb
1 kg (2 lb 4 oz) tomatoes, peeled
Salt and freshly ground pepper
150 ml (¼ pt) white wine

Put half the olive oil in casserole, add the onions, garlic, herbs and sweat for 5 minutes without colouring. Add the whole peeled tomatoes and simmer gently for 15 minutes. Add some white wine according to the juice of the tomatoes. Meanwhile, cook the peppers in the remaining olive oil until soft. Do the same with the courgettes, and again with the aubergines, but keep them still hard so they don't reduce into puree. Add all the 3 vegetables to the tomato coulis, reheat and season with lots of black pepper and salt. The more you reheat the ratatouille, the better it will taste!

Regis and Martine Crepy
The Great House Hotel and
Restaurant, Lavenham, Suffolk

BORTSCH (BORSCH OR BORSHCH)

Serves 6

1 onion, sliced or chopped
1 parsnip, sliced or chopped
1 carrot, sliced or chopped
1 raw beet, shredded
60 g (2 oz) cabbage, shredded
*1.2 ltrs (2 pts) stock (chicken or to
    your taste)*
2 tbsp tomato puree
1 dsp vinegar
1 bayleaf
1 tbsp sugar
60 g (2 oz) fat or oil
Salt and pepper
300 ml (½ pt) soured cream

Fry vegetables for a few minutes, stirring. Pour on the stock, add puree and vinegar. Season with salt, pepper and sugar.

Simmer for about 20 minutes until tender. Remove bayleaf. Sieve or liquidise.

Serve with a spoonful of sour cream or yoghurt and garnish with chopped parsley or chives. If necessary, thin with more stock.

Lorna Waller
Lavenham

Main Courses

Flemish Beef 20

Cheddar Cheese Pie 20

Barbeque Chicken 20

Lamb Cutlets en
Casserole 21

Hungarian Fricassee 21

Cotswold Rabbit Pie 21

Coronation Chicken 22

Chicken Breasts with
Mustard Sauce 22

Casseroled Pheasant 22

Spring Lamb Casserole 23

Root Vegetable Stew 23

Lamb 'Nicoes' 24

Baked Chicken with
Apricot Sauce 24

Stir-fried Pork with
Pineapple 24

Breast of Lamb in
Wine and Tarragon 25

Steak and Ale Pie 25

Pork Escalopes with
Mushrooms and
Mozzarella 26

Mediterranean Cassoulet 26

Liver with Apricots 27

Downland Lamb Fillet
with Garlic Sauce 27

Confit of Duck 28

Hot Rocket Capricorn
Cheesecake 28

Trout in Tomato Sauce
with Noodles 29

Faisan Strasbourgeois 29

Chicken and Broccoli
Lasagne 30

Crispy Roast Potatoes 30

FLEMISH BEEF

Serves 4

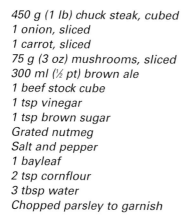

450 g (1 lb) chuck steak, cubed
1 onion, sliced
1 carrot, sliced
75 g (3 oz) mushrooms, sliced
300 ml (½ pt) brown ale
1 beef stock cube
1 tsp vinegar
1 tsp brown sugar
Grated nutmeg
Salt and pepper
1 bayleaf
2 tsp cornflour
3 tbsp water
Chopped parsley to garnish

Brown the steak in a frying pan and place in a 1¾ ltr (3 pts) casserole.

Add the onion, carrot and mushrooms. Blend the ale with the stock cube, vinegar, brown sugar and nutmeg, salt and pepper to taste. Pour over the meat and vegetables. Add the bayleaf.

Cover and cook in a pre-heated moderate oven 170°C, 325°F, Gas Mark 3, for about 2 hours or until the meat is tender. Mix the cornflour with the water and stir into the casserole. Cook for 15–20 minutes. Serve garnished with chopped parsley.

This dish is even tastier if made a day before it is required, and then re-heated. Very useful for busy cooks.

Daphne Robinson
Lavenham

CHEDDAR CHEESE PIE

6–8 slices of white bread
175 g (6 oz) Cheddar cheese
2 medium eggs
600 ml (1 pt) milk
Salt and pepper to taste

Pre-heat oven to 190°C, 375°F, Gas Mark 5. Crumble the bread into a mixing bowl (without the crusts). Grate the cheese on top, then warm the milk and beat the eggs into the milk. Pour the mixture over the bread and cheese and mix well together. Cook for 1 hour or until nice and brown. Serve with braised celery, jacket potato or a green salad.

Joan Lawrence Veazey
Lavenham

BARBEQUE CHICKEN

Place 4 chicken pieces in a roasting tin, cover with foil and bake at 350°C, 180°F, Gas Mark 4, for 1 hour. Meanwhile "plump" 2 oz of raisins in a little boiling water. Peel and chop 1 medium onion and fry in 1 oz of butter until soft. Add the drained raisins along with 3 tbsp each of Lyles Golden Syrup, tomato ketchup and brown sauce and, if you like, a few shakes of Worcester sauce. Season with salt, pepper and a pinch of mustard and let simmer until the syrup melts. Now pour the sauce over the chicken and bake uncovered for 15–20 minutes in pre-heated oven as above.

Yvonne Carr
Lavenham

LAMB CUTLETS EN CASSEROLE

Fill a casserole with alternate layers of chopped, skinned, tomatoes mixed with whole mushrooms (or sliced green peppers) and lamb cutlets. Season each layer – top and bottom ones should be vegetables. Top with small knobs of butter. Cook for 2–3 hours 150°C, 300°F, Gas Mark 2. Allow to get cold – remove fat. Reheat and serve.

Use ingredients according to number of servings.

Jane Bean
Lavenham

HUNGARIAN FRICASSEE

Serves 2

225 g (8 oz) veal cut into strips
2 tbsp flour mixed with 2 tbsp
   paprika
125 g (4 oz) mushrooms, sliced
1 onion, chopped
1 garlic clove, crushed
300 ml (½ pt) white wine
3 tbsp double cream
Chopped parsley
Salt and pepper to taste

Coat veal in flour and paprika and fry until brown on both sides. Add mushrooms, onion and garlic; cook until soft. Stir in wine, cover and simmer gently for 20 minutes. Stir in cream just before serving. Sprinkle chopped parsley on top. Serve on a bed of rice.

Pam Hardy
Lavenham

COTSWOLD RABBIT PIE

Serves 4

1 rabbit jointed, approximately
   1 kg (2½ lb)
2–3 tbsp seasoned flour
1 tbsp each oil and butter
125 g (4 oz) streaky bacon, cut in
   pieces
1 large onion, sliced
2 carrots, sliced
600 ml (1 pt) beef stock
A glass of red wine or port
½ tsp dried thyme or marjoram
125 g (4 oz) mushrooms, sliced
4 thick slices of bread
Leaf parsley to garnish

Dip the rabbit joints in the seasoned flour. Heat the oil in a large pan and fry on all sides with the bacon until brown, then transfer into an oven-proof casserole.

Add the onions and carrots to the pan, stir around for a couple of minutes and pour over the stock and wine. Bring to the boil, add the herbs, season well and pour over the meat. Cover and cook at 180°C, 350°F, Gas Mark 4, for 1–1½ hours, then add the sliced mushrooms.

Cut the bread into triangles, dip into the gravy and place gravy side up, overlapping in the top of the casserole. Cook, uncovered, for a further 30 minutes until the bread is crisp. Sprinkle with chopped parsley and serve with braised red cabbage.

Celia Goodrick-Clarke
Cookery Writer, Daily Mail

CORONATION CHICKEN

4 chicken breasts (on bone)
2 tbsp oil
1 small onion, finely chopped
2 tbsp mango chutney
2 tsp tomato puree
150 ml (¼ pt) chicken stock made
    with half chicken oxo
300 ml (½ pt) mayonnaise
2 tbsp cream (any kind)
Approximately 2 tbsp curry
    powder (medium or hot)

Remove skins from chicken. Boil and simmer for 20–30 minutes until tender. Remove meat from bone and allow to get cold. Break into bite size pieces.

Soften onion in oil. Add curry powder. Stir fry for 2 minutes. Add chutney, puree and stock. Simmer for 5 minutes.

Allow to cool (then strain if desired). When cold, stir in cream and mayonnaise. Pour over chicken. Serve with boiled rice.

Maureen Roberts
Lavenham

CHICKEN BREASTS WITH MUSTARD SAUCE

4 chicken breasts (skinless)
125 g (4 oz) seedless grapes

Mustard sauce
150 ml (¼ pt) single cream
1 tbsp wholegrain mustard
3 tbsp mayonnaise

Take chicken breasts and place in a lidded casserole. Add grapes, which are cut in half, then add the mustard sauce. Cook for 1½ hours 190°C, 375°F, Gas Mark 5, turning chicken once.

Serve with fresh vegetables and croquette potatoes – and a glass of white wine!

Doreen Brinkley
Lavenham

CASSEROLED PHEASANT

2 pheasants
6–8 shallots
25 g (1 oz) butter
125 g (4 oz) streaky bacon
125 g (4 oz) mushrooms, chopped
1 tbsp mixed herbs
½ tbsp fresh chopped thyme
Small wine glass of sherry (not
    sweet) and port

Cut and fry pheasant and shallots in butter. Cut up streaky bacon and add with mushrooms. Add a pinch of mixed herbs and add fresh thyme, also sherry, port and chicken stock cube. Simmer on cooker hob for 1½ hours, or until tender.

If desired, add cornflour, gravy salt and Bisto for a thicker or darker gravy.

Doreen Brinkley
Lavenham

SPRING LAMB CASSEROLE

25 g (1 oz) seasoned flour
900–1125 g (2–2½ lb) boned shoulder
   of lamb, cubed (I use fillet)
3 tbsp oil
225 g (8 oz) onions, peeled and
   sliced
300 ml (½ pt) orange juice
600 ml (1 pt) lamb stock
450 g (1 lb) carrots, peeled and
   sliced
25 g (1 oz) sultanas
75 g (3 oz) apricots, halved and
   soaked
Salt and pepper to taste

Pre-heat oven to 180°C, 350°F,
Gas Mark 4.

Toss meat in seasoned flour.
Heat oil in large pan and fry
meat until browned. Remove
meat from pan and fry onion
until golden. Return meat to pan,
add orange juice and stock.

Bring to the boil, stirring all
the time. Add carrots, sultanas
and apricots. Cook in casserole
until tender, 2–2½ hours. Add
seasoning to taste.

Coral Allworthy, Lavenham

ROOT VEGETABLE STEW

450 g (1 lb) quality stewing beef,
   cubed
1 tbsp olive oil
1 onion or 2 leeks, sliced
2 garlic cloves (optional)
4 rashers bacon, sliced
400 g (14 oz) tin chopped
   tomatoes
450–1 kg (1–2 lb) root vegetables,
   such as parsnip, swede, celeriac
   or celery, carrots, turnip, cut into
   even chunks
300 ml (½ pt) each wine and beef
   stock
Seasoning to taste

Brown the meat on all sides in the
hot oil, scoop out and put in a
casserole. Add the bacon, onion
or leeks and garlic to the pan
and saute for 3–4 minutes, pour
in the tomatoes and add the root
vegetables.

Allow to soften for about 5
minutes, season to taste and add
the wine and enough stock to cover
the vegetables. Bring to the boil
and pour over the meat. Cover and
cook for 2 hours at 160°C, 325°F,
Gas Mark 3, or until the meat is
tender.

For the dumplings: Make the
dumplings by combining 175 g (6 oz)
self-raising flour, 1 tsp mustard
powder, pinch dried herbs, 2 tbsp
chopped fresh parsley and 75 g
(3 oz) shredded suet in a bowl and
adding enough cold water to make
a soft, but not sticky dough. Divide
into 8 small balls with floured
fingers. Place on top of the meat
and vegetables (do not submerge)
replace the lid and cook for a
further 15–20 minutes.

Lighter cheesy dumplings: Sieve
200 g (7 oz) flour with 2 tsp baking
powder and 1 tsp salt. Add 4 tbsp
grated Parmesan cheese and 2–3
tbsp chopped fresh parsley. Mix 1
egg into the mixture with just
enough milk to make a soft (but not
sticky) dough. Form into 8 small
balls. To serve, chopped fresh
parsley and dumplings.

Celia Goodrick-Clarke
Cookery Writer, Daily Mail

LAMB 'NICOES'

This works so well in textures and flavours.

1 x 200 g (7 oz) chump lamb
10 fine beans
4 cherry tomatoes
8 stoned olives
1 hard boiled egg
3 peeled new potatoes
3 oz herbs, chopped

Roast chump lamb to your liking. Cook potatoes and keep hot. Cook fine beans and refresh in iced water when cooked. Peel hard boiled egg and cut into quarters. When lamb is ready mix in a bowl beans, tomatoes, olives, herbs, egg and warm potatoes. Season with olive oil. Place ingredients in a bowl and place sliced lamb on top and serve.

Jason Buck, Head Chef
The Swan Hotel, Lavenham

BAKED CHICKEN WITH APRICOT SAUCE

Chicken pieces (according to
    needs!)
1 pkt French onion soup
1 medium tin apricot puree

Put chicken in oven-proof dish. Sprinkle over soup mixture and apricot puree. Bake in oven 180°C, 350°F, Gas Mark 4, for 45 minutes.

If cooking a large quantity, increase cooking time.

Anne Jones
Lavenham

STIR-FRIED PORK WITH PINEAPPLE

Serves 4

450 g (1 lb) lean pork, cut into thin
    strips
4 tbsp cooking oil
1 green pepper, cut into ½ inch strips
¼ tsp ground ginger
1 large onion, chopped
3 tbsp soy sauce
2 tbsp wine vinegar
200 g (7 oz) tin of pineapple
    chunks (reserve the juice)
225 g (8 oz) tin of water chestnuts,
    sliced (optional)
3 tsp cornflour blended in 2 tbsp
    water

Stir-fry the pork in 2 tbsp of oil for 5–7 minutes. Remove from pan, add the remaining oil. Stir-fry the onion and green pepper for 2 minutes.

Return pork to the pan. Reduce heat and stir in ginger, soy sauce and wine vinegar. Add the pineapple chunks and make up the juice to 300 ml (½ pt) with water.

Add to the pan (with water chestnuts if used). Stir in the blended cornflour and water. Bring to the boil, stirring, and serve with rice.

Paulton Women's Fellowship
Paulton, Somerset

BREAST OF LAMB IN WINE AND TARRAGON

Serves 2

Marinate lamb overnight

1 lamb breast, chopped into
*   cubes*
1 dsp chopped or dried tarragon
2 tbsp red wine
1 bouquet garni

1 onion
2 tbsp tomato paste
3 tomatoes, skinned and chopped
1 tbsp paprika
300 ml (½ pt) vegetable stock
Salt and pepper to taste

Trim fat from breast of lamb and lightly fry, then place in casserole dish.

Liquidise onion and tomatoes with marinade, add all other ingredients and cover lamb. Place dish on middle shelf of oven 180°C, 350°F, Gas Mark 4 for 1 hour. Add 1 dsp of cream or yoghurt before serving.

Pam Hardy
Lavenham

STEAK AND ALE PIE

Serves 27! – makes 3 large pies

4½ kg (10 lb) diced lean stewing
*   steak*
4 large onions
2 ltrs (3½ pts) beef stock
2 ltrs (3½ pts) dark bitter
6 tbsp brown sugar
Salt and pepper to taste
Beurre manie (or cornflour to
*   thicken sauce)*

Pastry
570 g (20 oz) self-raising flour
285 g (10 oz) shredded beef suet
Salt and pepper
A little water

Brown the beef in a large pan with a little oil or lard. Chop the onions and stir these into the beef and allow to soften. Add the stock, bitter, sugar, and season with salt and pepper and bring to the boil. Lower the heat and simmer gently until the beef is tender (3–3½ hours). Remove the beef with a slotted spoon and thicken the sauce by gradually whisking in the beurre manie (or cornflour) over a moderate heat.

Combine the flour, suet, salt and pepper in a large bowl. Carefully mix in the water so that the mixture just holds together without being sticky and leave to rest for 5 minutes.

Fill a pie dish with the meat and sauce mixture and cover with the rolled out pastry. Decorate as required and brush with beaten egg.

Bake in a moderate oven 180°C, 350°F, Gas Mark 4, until the pastry is cooked, about 25 minutes.

Ray and Anne Whitworth
John and Val Barry
The Angel
Lavenham
Suffolk

■ *This recipe works well for smaller quantities – using a third of quantities given for the larger pies, and it tastes delicious.*

Evelyn Curtis

PORK ESCALOPES WITH MUSHROOMS AND MOZZARELLA

Serves 4

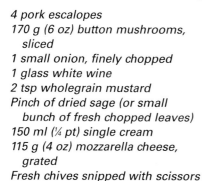

4 pork escalopes
170 g (6 oz) button mushrooms, sliced
1 small onion, finely chopped
1 glass white wine
2 tsp wholegrain mustard
Pinch of dried sage (or small bunch of fresh chopped leaves)
150 ml (¼ pt) single cream
115 g (4 oz) mozzarella cheese, grated
Fresh chives snipped with scissors

Saute the chopped onion in a little olive oil until softened. Add the sage and mushrooms and continue cooking for 2 minutes. Pour in white wine and reduce by half. Add cream, bring to the boil and simmer until sauce is fairly thick (usually 1 minute).

Remove from the heat, season with a little salt and pepper and stir in whole grain mustard. Keep warm.

Add a little cooking oil to a large frying pan, coat both sides of the pork escalopes in seasoned flour and place in the hot pan one at a time. Cook for 2 minutes either side. As they are cooked, place onto a warm baking sheet and keep warm until all are cooked and you are ready to add the sauce.

Spread the mushroom sauce over the escalopes, with grated mozzarella and put under a hot grill to allow the cheese to bubble and brown. Sprinkle with snipped fresh chives and serve.

Roy and Anne Whitworth
John and Val Barry
The Angel
Lavenham
Suffolk

MEDITERRANEAN CASSOULET

Serves 4

4 tbsp extra virgin olive oil
1 onion, chopped
2 cloves garlic, crushed
1 red and 1 yellow pepper, diced
1 aubergine and 2 courgettes, diced
1 tbsp tomato puree
4 tomatoes, peeled and chopped
½ tbsp brown sugar
½ tsp harissa paste (or to taste)
900 ml (1½ pts) vegetable stock
120 ml (4 fl oz) dry white wine
125 g (4 oz) both haricot beans and brown lentils, soaked overnight and drained
1 tbsp chopped fresh rosemary, 1 bayleaf and ¼ tsp fennel seeds

Cook the onion and garlic in the hot oil for 1–2 minutes. Add the peppers, aubergine and courgettes and cook for 8–10 minutes.

Stir in the tomato puree, tomatoes, sugar and harissa and cook for a further 5 minutes. Add wine, stock, beans, lentils and herbs and bring to the boil.

Transfer to an oven-proof dish, cover and cook for 1 hour at 160°C, 325°F, Gas Mark 3.

Celia Goodrick-Clarke
Cookery Writer
Daily Mail

LIVER WITH APRICOTS

425 g (15 oz) tin apricots
Good pinch mixed herbs
Pinch of mustard powder
1 dsp soy sauce
Grated zest of ½ lemon
1 tbsp natural yoghurt
4 to 6 slices of Liver

Put all ingredients, except the liver, into a blender and blend. Place liver in a dish and pour all the blended ingredients over the liver. Cover with foil and bake for 40 minutes, 190°C, 375°F, Gas Mark 5. After 40 minutes take out and coat liver with 125 g (4 oz) breadcrumbs and 75 g (3 oz) grated cheese, return to dish, cover, bake for a further 10 minutes.

Paul Dugget, Lavenham

DOWNLAND LAMB FILLET WITH GARLIC SAUCE

A wonderfully simple yet delicious alternative to a Sunday roast or dinner party favourite.
Serves 4–6

685 g (1½ lb) lamb fillet from the
    loin
15 g (½ oz) butter
4 sprigs of thyme
Salt and freshly ground black
    pepper

Garlic sauce
20 cloves garlic, unpeeled
200 ml (7 fl oz) milk
30 g (1 oz) butter
1 tbsp sugar
430 ml (15 fl oz) lamb or chicken
    stock
285 ml (10 fl oz) creme fraiche

Season the lamb fillet with salt and pepper. Rub all over with butter and thyme leaves, pressing them into the meat. Place in the roasting tin and leave to stand for 20 minutes.

Cook, uncovered for 15–20 minutes at 200°C, 400°F, Gas Mark 6. If preferred slightly more well done, cook for another 10 minutes. Remove and allow to rest.

To make garlic sauce, place the garlic cloves together with the milk in the saucepan, bring to the boil and cook for 5 minutes on the simmering plate. Drain and discard the milk.

Place the garlic cloves, still unpeeled back into the saucepan and add the butter and sugar. Saute until light golden brown. Allow the garlic to cool then peel and chop finely. All this may seem a bit of a fuss, but it really is worth it. The boiling in milk takes away all the bitterness and the sauteeing adds richness and sweetness to the garlic. Place this chopped garlic in a saucepan with the stock and creme fraiche and bring to the boil. Transfer to the simmering plate and slowly reduce until it becomes a light creamy consistency. Pour through a sieve, pushing through as much garlic as possible.

Carve the lamb into thin slices, spoon a little sauce onto each plate, arrange slices of lamb and spoon over a little more sauce.

Garnish with fresh mint and serve with tiny new potatoes.

**Bernadette Fraser and Ann Brewer
Authors of the Barn House Aga
Cookbook**

CONFIT OF DUCK

Serves 4

2 medium sized ducks
1 tbsp sea salt
1 ltr (approx. 1¾ pts) goose fat
2–3 bayleaves
2–3 springs thyme

Take only the legs and wings for this recipe (leave the breast for another recipe).

Put the salt, crumbled bayleaves, thyme and pepper onto the pieces of duck and let it rest for a minimum of 4 hours.

Remove the excess salt and put the duck pieces into a casserole. Cover with goose fat and cook slowly for about 3 hours 150°C, 300°F, Gas Mark 2, making sure the fat does not boil. When cooked you should be able to take the meat off the bone effortlessly.

To serve, put the pieces in the oven and let them brown for about 15 minutes. Serve with green vegetables and roasted potatoes.

Regis and Martine Crepy
The Great House Hotel and
Restaurant
Lavenham, Suffolk

HOT ROCKET
CAPRICORN CHEESECAKE

Base
175 g (6 oz) biscuits (we make our
    own oatcakes and poppyseed
    crackers which we use for more
    depth of flavour)
50 g (2 oz) mixed seeds (sesame,
    poppyseed and pumpkin)
50 g (2 oz) butter

Cake
2 red onions, sliced
25 g (1 oz) butter
450 g (1 lb) rocket leaves
225 g (8 oz) cream cheese
225 g (8 oz) vegetarian rennet
    goat's cheese eg. Capricorn or
    Ragstone
290 g (10–11 oz) carton soured
    cream
4 free range eggs, lightly beaten
Seasoning

Pre-heat oven to 180°C, 350°F, Gas Mark 4. Line the base of a 9 inch spring form tin with greaseproof paper and lightly grease the sides.

Melt the butter for the base (easiest in microwave) and stir seeds and biscuit crumbs in it. Press mixture evenly over base of prepared tin. Refrigerate.

In a large pan melt the "cake" butter and fry the onion slices for approximately 4 minutes until softened. Add the rocket to the pan and cover with lid and cook (approximately 2½ minutes).

Remove from heat and stir in cheeses and sour cream. Stir in eggs and season. Pour mixture over the base and bake for approximately 1 hour until firm and golden.

Serve hot with warmed sundried tomatoes drizzled with basil and garlic dressing – Mmmm . . . . delicious!

Les and Vanessa Scott
Strattons Hotel
Swaffham
Norfolk

TROUT IN TOMATO SAUCE WITH NOODLES

This dish is quick and easy to prepare and can be on the table in under 20 minutes.

350 g (12 oz) flat noodles
3 tbsp olive oil
50 g (2 oz) polyunsaturated
  margarine
1 large onion, finely chopped
1 large garlic clove, finely
  chopped
225 g (8 oz) mushrooms, sliced
4 trout fillets, skinned and roughly
  diced
1 tbsp tomato puree
275 ml (½ pt) low fat creme fraiche
Salt
Freshly ground black pepper
2 tbsp fresh basil, chopped

Bring some water to the boil in a large saucepan. Add the noodles and boil for 11–12 minutes. When just soft drain, mix in 1 tbsp of the olive oil and place on a warm serving dish.

Meanwhile in a large deep frying pan, melt the margarine with the remaining olive oil. Add the onion and garlic and fry until the onion is just tender. Add the mushrooms and cook until soft.

Stir in the trout, tomato puree and creme fraiche and simmer for about 5 minutes. Season with salt and pepper and stir in basil. Pour sauce over noodles. Serve with crusty bread and a side salad.

**Evelyn Curtis
Lavenham**

■ *My Monthly Cookery Article, February 1999. Courtesy of the Somerset Magazine, Crewkerne.*

FAISAN STRASBOURGEOIS

Take a pheasant, preferably a young hen and, rather than pluck it, skin it, thereby removing all the feathers and the skin in one go. This can be achieved relatively easily by inserting a pair of scissors in the obvious place and cutting up the breastbone, then pulling off the skin and feathers. It is advisable to chop off the ends of the wings and the head before starting.

Remove the innards, retaining on one side the giblets for the sauce.

Place the skinned bird in a cast-iron stewing pot and cover with 600 ml (1 pt) of juice made of two thirds chicken or game stock and one third white wine, to which you add the cleaned giblets. Add root vegetables cut in large chunks. Cover and simmer until the flesh is tender.

Remove the bird and the vegetables and keep warm.

Strain the juice and season it, and then add 300 ml (½ pt) yoghurt and 3 tbsp of coarse-grained mustard. Bring to the boil, simmer and reduce by a third.

Carve the bird into large pieces and arrange the vegetables around each serving. Pour the sauce over.

Very useful in January when roast pheasant has become very familiar.

**The Earl of Stockton
Chairman, Macmillan Publishers**

CHICKEN AND BROCCOLI LASAGNE

*This makes a tasty main meal or supper dish
with a salad and French loaf.*

*50 g (2 oz) butter
1 onion, sliced
50 g (2 oz) flour
850 ml (1½ pts) milk
1 chicken stock cube
350 g (12 oz) cooked chicken, diced
225 g (8 oz) small broccoli florets,
    blanched
100 g (4 oz) sweetcorn
1 tsp dried mixed herbs
Freshly ground pepper
8 sheets ready-to-cook lasagne
50 g (2 oz) Red Leicester cheese,
    grated*

Melt butter and fry onion for 5 minutes. Stir in flour and cook for 2 minutes. Gradually stir in milk and stock cube. Heat, stirring continuously until the sauce thickens, boils and is smooth. Cook for 2–3 minutes. Remove from heat, add chicken, broccoli, sweetcorn, herbs and seasoning.

Place a thin layer of the sauce in base of a greased 25½ x 20½ cm (10 x 8 inch) oven-proof dish. Cover with 4 sheets of lasagne.

Repeat layers of sauce and lasagne once more ending with a layer of sauce. Sprinkle with cheese and bake at 190°C, 375°F, Gas Mark 5, for 35 minutes.

**Jean Boyd
Lavenham**

CRISPY ROAST POTATOES

There is nothing more delicious than crispy roast potatoes served with good English beef and a few choice vegetables.

The problem is that often the potatoes turn out to be soggy when they ought to be absolutely crunchy.

Here is an unfailing recipe for the best roast potatoes you have ever tasted.

Take any good red-skinned potatoes, peel them and cut into manageable portions if necessary and boil gently for 10–12 minutes.

Drain off the water and gently shake in pan to make them 'floury'.

Whilst the potatoes are boiling place a suitable quantity of olive oil in a shallow baking tin and heat the oven.

When the oil is hot, remove from oven and place the baking tray over a flame so that the oil remains hot.

Place each potato in the hot oil and gently baste with the oil. Return the baking tin to the oven and cook along with the roast beef, but on no account place the roast potatoes around the beef.

Baste the potatoes from time to time. The real secret of getting crispy roast potatoes is to ensure the oil remains hot when you place the potatoes in it for the first time.

**This recipe was kindly sent
to me by Terry Waite, CBE
Hartest, Suffolk**

Puddings

Double Lemon Pudding 32

Marshmallow Flan 32

Orange and Honey Bananas 32

Chocolate Layer Pudding 33

Iced Caramel Mousse 33

Black Forest Trifle 33

Naughty Pudding 34

Fruit Pot 34

Pavlova 34

Strawberry Tartlets 35

Chilled Lemon Flan 35

Mandarin Mousse 35

Brandy Bombe 36

Chocolate Surprise 36

Rhubarb and Ginger Compote 36

Syllabub Trifle 37

Coffee Flan 37

Apricot Pudding 38

Tipsy Trifle 38

Coconut Pie 38

Oatmeal Crunch 39

Chocolate Fudge Pudding 39

Banana Creme Brulee 39

Chocolate Truffle Fantasy 40

Butterscotch Pudding 40

Rummy Bananas 40

Kirsch Cream Ice with Compote of Berries 41

Yoghurt Icecream 41

Blackcurrant Cheesecake 42

DOUBLE LEMON PUDDING

4 eggs, separated
350 g (12 oz) caster sugar
425 ml (¾ pt) milk
15–25 g (¾ oz) plain flour
Juice and zest of 2 lemons

Beat egg yolks and sugar, add lemon juice, zest, milk and flour, then fold in whisked egg whites. Pour into a buttered dish and place in a dish or tin of warm water 180°C, 350°F, Gas Mark 4, for 45 minutes.

Eileen Huffey
Lavenham

MARSHMALLOW FLAN

Biscuit crust
115 g (4 oz) digestive biscuits, crushed
60 g (2 oz) melted butter
2 small tsp brown sugar

Filling
115 g (4 oz) marshmallows
¾ breakfast cup milk
Dash of vanilla essence or other flavouring
½ cup of double cream
2 egg whites

Crush biscuits with rolling pin, finely, and place in a basin. Melt butter with the sugar and pour over. Press mixture well down and round the sides of a fairly deep flan dish. Put aside to cool for an hour.

Melt marshmallows in the milk and flavouring; leave to cool and beginning to set. Add stiffly whipped cream and egg whites and pour into biscuit lined dish. It will not set too firm, but it will not be too runny either! Decorate with chocolate or nuts.

Jill Niemeyer
Lavenham

ORANGE AND HONEY BANANAS

Serves 4

2–3 oranges
4 firm bananas
2 tbsp honey
2 tbsp Grand Marnier (optional)
Low fat fromage frais to serve

Pre-heat oven to 200°C, 400°F, Gas Mark 6.

Grate rind and squeeze juice from 2 of the oranges. If you wish to decorate the dish when it is completed, pare the other orange with a canelle knife and cut into slices.

Peel bananas and cut them in half lengthways. Place them in an oven-proof dish. Place the rind and orange juice in a pan with the honey. Heat through until the honey has dissolved. Pour the liquid over the bananas and cover the dish with foil. Place in the oven and bake for 15–20 minutes. Remove from oven and stir in the Grand Marnier (if using). Serve hot with fromage frais.

Norma Pratt
Lavenham

CHOCOLATE LAYER PUDDING

No cooking!

115 g (4 oz) brown breadcrumbs
115 g (4 oz) chocolate, grated
85 g (3 oz) demerara sugar

Mix together. Whip large carton 300 ml (½ pt)) double or whipping cream.

Put ½ inch layers of crumb mixture and the cream in a glass souffle dish, finishing with cream. Sprinkle with grated chocolate.

Jane Bean
Lavenham

ICED CARAMEL MOUSSE

3 Mars bars
300 ml (½ pt) double cream
1 tbsp milk
1 egg white

Thinly slice Mars bars. Place in a bowl with the milk, stand this over a pan of simmering water.

Heat gently, stirring until melted. Cool for about 10 minutes, stirring occasionally. Whisk cream until it holds its shape. Stir a large spoonful of cream into caramel mixture. Then fold in remaining cream.

Lightly whisk egg white, and fold into the chocolate mixture. Pour into bowl, cover and freeze for 2–3 hours before serving, decorate with chocolate curls. Will keep in freezer. Allow to thaw before serving.

Mary Holland
Lavenham

BLACK FOREST TRIFLE

Serves 6

1 chocolate Swiss roll
3 tbsp Kirsch
425 g (15 oz) can black cherries, drained and stoned
3 egg yolks
1 tbsp cornflour
25 g (1 oz) caster sugar
425 ml (¾ pt) milk
¼ tsp almond essence
150 ml (5 fl oz) whipped double cream
Fresh black cherries to decorate, or reserved ones from can (optional)

Slice Swiss roll into dish, sprinkle with Kirsch and cherries. Cream egg yolks with cornflour and sugar. Bring milk to boil, pour onto eggs, stir well. Return to pan stirring continuously until mixture coats the back of a wooden spoon. Add almond essence, pour over cherries and leave to cool.

Spread three quarters of the cream over the custard. Pipe the rest into rosettes over the top (or use all the cream to spread over the top of the custard). Decorate with remaining cherries.

St. Peter's Wives Group
Paulton, Somerset

NAUGHTY PUDDING

1 pkt chocolate chip cookies
2 wine glasses of sherry
1 medium carton ready made
 custard
150 ml (¼ pt) double cream
100 g (3 oz) bar Cadbury's Dairy
 Milk Chocolate
1 Cadbury's Flake

Arrange half the cookies in the bottom of serving dish and pour over half the sherry. Place remaining cookies in another dish and pour over remaining sherry. Melt chocolate in a basin and allow to cool slightly. Spoon 4–5 tbsp custard into chocolate and mix well. Spread chocolate mixture over biscuits in serving dish. Place remaining cookies on top of chocolate mixture. Whisk cream until thick, but "floppy". Fold cream and remaining custard together and spread evenly over biscuit mixture. Crumble flake and sprinkle on top.

Refrigerate until needed. Can be made the day before.

Vickie Weaver
Lavenham

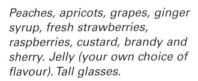

FRUIT POT

Peaches, apricots, grapes, ginger syrup, fresh strawberries, raspberries, custard, brandy and sherry. Jelly (your own choice of flavour). Tall glasses.

Fill glasses with fruits, peaches, apricots, grapes, and add ginger. Also add a little brandy and sherry.

Cover with jelly and leave to set. When ready, add fresh fruit, strawberries, raspberries, or any fresh fruit available. Just before serving, fill glasses with cold custard and top with a strawberry.

Doreen Brinkley
Lavenham

PAVLOVA

This is a perfect pudding for a dinner party.

4 egg whites
225 g (8 oz) caster sugar
½ tsp vanilla essence
1 tsp vinegar
1 tsp cornflour

Draw an 8 inch circle on non-stick paper and place it on a baking tray.

Whisk egg whites until stiff and standing in peaks. Beat in the sugar, 1 tbsp at a time. Fold in the vanilla essence, vinegar and cornflour.

Spoon the meringue mixture over the round on the non-stick paper, making a slight hollow in the centre. Bake in a low oven 130°C, 250°F, Gas Mark ½, for 1 hour until firm.

Leave to cool, carefully remove the non-stick paper. Place on a serving plate and fill the hollow with 300 ml (½ pt) whipped cream and 225 g (8 oz) raspberries or strawberries.

Renée Attew, Lavenham

STRAWBERRY TARTLETS

175 g (6 oz) rich shortcrust pastry
Sugar to taste
225 g (8 oz) cream cheese
A little cream
225 g (8 oz) small strawberries
150 ml (¼ pt) redcurrant jelly

Roll out the prepared pastry thinly and with a cutter cut into 2 inch rounds. Bake blind for about 8 minutes at 191°C, 375°F, Gas Mark 5. When they are golden brown take from the oven and cool on wire tray. Add sugar to taste to the cream cheese, and if this is a little dry, add enough cream to moisten it.

When tartlets are cold fill with cream cheese and arrange the strawberries on top. Beat jelly until smooth and heat it just a little, but do not let it boil. Brush this over the strawberries.

The amount of redcurrant jelly should be sufficient to fill the tartlets and hold the strawberries firmly in place.

Well worth a little time and effort, as they look professional when finished.

**Evelyn Curtis
Lavenham**

CHILLED LEMON FLAN

Flan case
115 g (4 oz) digestive biscuits
60 g (2 oz) butter
1 level tbsp caster sugar

Filling
150 ml (¼ pt) double cream
175 g (6 oz) can condensed milk
2 large lemons and juice

Topping
Lightly whipped double cream
Fresh or crystallised lemon slices

Crush digestive biscuits. Melt butter in a pan. Add sugar then blend in biscuit crumbs. Mix well and turn mixture into 7 inch pie plate or flan dish and press into

shape around base and sides with the back of a spoon. Bake in a slow oven (130°C, 250°F, Gas Mark ½) for 8–10 minutes. Remove from oven and leave to cool. Do not turn flan case out of dish as it will crumble.

Mix together cream, condensed milk and finely grated lemon rind. Slowly beat in lemon juice. Pour mixture into flan case and chill for several hours until firm.

Just before serving, decorate with lightly whipped cream and lemon slices.

**Jean Hillman
Paulton, Somerset**

MANDARIN MOUSSE

1 tangerine or orange jelly
1 small tin mandarins
1 small tin condensed milk

Make jelly up with 300 ml (½ pt) water. Add fruit juice to make the jelly up to 425 ml (¾ pt). Put milk

into trifle dish and whisk for 5–10 minutes. Add cooled jelly and whisk again. Add fruit and chill until set.

**St. Peter's Wives Group
Paulton, Somerset**

BRANDY BOMBE

A rich dessert, popular with friends and relatives,
and so easy to prepare in advance.
Serves 4

300 ml (½ pt) double cream
2 tbsp brandy
1 tbsp caster sugar
115 g (4 oz) meringue, roughly
broken

Whisk cream until stiff and stir in the brandy and caster sugar. Fold in the broken meringue pieces. Add extra caster sugar and/or brandy for individual taste. Put mixture into lightly oiled 600 ml (1 pt) pudding basin. Cover, seal and freeze. Unmould just before serving, or put in fridge for 15 minutes. Decorate with raspberries or serve with melba sauce if required.

The Revd. Derrick Stiff
Rector of Lavenham

CHOCOLATE SURPRISE

Serves 4–6

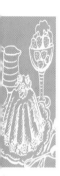

115 g (4 oz) breadcrumbs (brown
or white, but not granary)
115 g (4 oz) caster sugar
4 tbsp drinking chocolate
2 dsp coffee granules
600 ml (1 pt) whipping cream
(or creme fraiche, or
marscapone)

Whip the cream to a spreading consistency. Mix all dry ingredients together thoroughly. Using a deep glass dish, a souffle dish is ideal, layer the crumb mixture alternatively with the cream.

There should be sufficient for 2 layers of chocolate mixture and 2 of cream. Finish with cream on top. Refrigerate overnight. Ask your guests to guess the ingredients!

Jo Wright
Lavenham

RHUBARB AND GINGER COMPOTE

This compote is extremely good – the ginger gives just
the right flavour of spicy sweetness to the rhubarb.
Serves 4–6

450 g (1 lb) rhubarb
225 g (8 oz) caster sugar
450 ml (16 fl oz) water
2 tbsp ginger syrup or ½ tsp
ground ginger
1–2 tbsp thinly sliced preserved
ginger (optional)

Trim and cut rhubarb. Put sugar and water into a pan and boil rapidly for 5 minutes, add ginger syrup or powder, mixed with a little of the syrup from pan. Draw aside, add rhubarb, cover and poach gently for 5–7 minutes. Arrange rhubarb in a serving dish, pour over juice, and scatter with the sliced ginger. Chill before serving.

Evelyn Curtis
My May 1999 cookery article. Courtesy
of The Somerset Magazine, Crewkerne

SYLLABUB TRIFLE

Serves 8

1 large jam Swiss roll
Medium sweet sherry to taste
6 kiwi fruit
115 g (4 oz) macaroons
3 egg whites
115 g (4 oz) caster sugar
150 ml (¼ pt) dry white Vermouth
2 tbsp brandy
1 tbsp lemon juice
300 ml (½ pt) carton double cream
    or whipped cream
Tiny ratafias and slices of kiwi
    fruit for decoration

Early in the day slice the Swiss roll and arrange in a large trifle bowl. Moisten with some sherry. Peel and slice kiwi fruit. Place over Swiss roll with broken macaroons.

Whisk egg whites until stiff, then gradually beat in the sugar until firm and glossy.

Pour in the Vermouth, brandy and lemon juice and gently fold through the meringue.

Whip the cream separately to the floppy stage and fold through the meringue mixture.

Pour over Swiss roll and fruit, cover and refrigerate for about 2 hours.

To serve, decorate.

Carole Boreham
Lavenham

COFFEE FLAN

Base
115 g (4 oz) plain chocolate
    digestive biscuits
60 g (2 oz) butter

Filling
230 ml (8 fl oz) milk
2 tbsp ground coffee
2 eggs, separated
85 g (3 oz) soft brown sugar
Pinch of salt
1 tsp gelatine soaked in 3 tsp
    water

To finish
150 ml (¼ pt) double cream
Grated chocolate

Pre-heat oven 190°C, 375°F, Gas Mark 5.

Crush biscuits. Melt butter and add biscuit crumbs. Place 7–8 inch flan ring on baking tray. Press crumbs across the base and partly up side of the ring. Bake for 10 minutes. Allow to cool.

Bring milk to the boil, add ground coffee and allow to infuse for 15 minutes.

Beat together the egg yolks, sugar and salt until thick and light. Strain on the coffee flavoured milk, and cook over a low heat until mixture coats the back of spoon.

Stir in soaked gelatine and allow to cool. When the mixture begins to thicken fold in the stiffly whisked egg whites. Pour into the prepared biscuit base. (This flan freezes well, so freeze at this stage.)

When set, carefully remove flan ring. Whip the cream, flavour with a little vanilla essence (if desired). Spread roughly over the top of the flan. Decorate with a little grated chocolate.

Margaret Beverly
Lavenham

APRICOT PUDDING

Serves 4–6

Put 115 g (4 oz) dried apricots into a basin, cover with cold water and soak for 12 hours. Strain. Cut fruit into small pieces. Rub 115 g (4 oz) margarine into 4 heaped tbsp self-raising flour, add 4 heaped tbsp breadcrumbs, then apricots and 4 tbsp sugar. Stir in 1 beaten egg and sufficient milk to make a soft smooth mixture. Put into greased basin, cover with greased paper and steam for 1½ hours. Serve with custard.

Rosemary Wheeler, Cambridge

TIPSY TRIFLE

Every family has their own way of making a trifle, no two are ever the same. This recipe is my cheat's version, which I have down to such a fine art I can make it in 3½ minutes flat. It's a god-send at any time of year.

Serves 6–8

To make your own boozy cream, beat 2 tbsp brandy, Cointreau or whisky into 300 ml (10 fl oz) double cream
1 box trifle sponges or Boudour fingers
9 tbsp sherry
3 tbsp brandy
1 carton Marks & Spencer's Summer Fruit Compote or red fruit jam diluted with a little lemon juice
1 small box ratafia biscuits
1 carton good fresh custard
1–2 tubs brandy cream
Fresh or frozen raspberries, ratafia biscuits or flaked almonds to decorate

Layer the sponges evenly at the bottom of a pretty glass dish. Soak them in the brandy and sherry – add more booze if you think the sponges are still dry.

Spoon the fruit compote evenly over the sponges, then sprinkle on a handful of ratafia biscuits. Pour the custard over, smoothing the surface with the back of a spoon, then top with the cream.

To decorate, use fresh or frozen raspberries and ratafia biscuits or flaked almonds. Chill well for all the flavour to merge.

Celia Goodrick-Clarke
Cookery Writer, Daily Mail

■ *One word of warning – tipsy trifle is quite alcoholic, so it's only fair to warn anyone who is driving so they can make allowances.*

COCONUT PIE

Serves 6

1.2 ltrs (2 pts) double thick custard
60 g (2 oz) margarine
85 g (3 oz) desiccated coconut

Line a pie plate or dish with 225 g (8 oz) short pastry, bake at 180°C, 350°F, Gas Mark 4, and cool. Make custard, and while still warm beat in margarine. When cool beat again, adding desiccated coconut. Spoon into pastry case, leave to cool and decorate as desired.

Rosemary Wheeler, Cambridge

OATMEAL CRUNCH

A delicious and easy alternative topping for an apple crumble.
Serves 4–6

75 g (3 oz) rolled oats
60 g (2 oz) plain flour
5 tbsp demerara sugar
115 g (4 oz) butter

Mix the demerara sugar, flour and oats. Melt the butter in a saucepan, over a low heat. Take off the heat and add the dry ingredients and mix well. Spread over prepared stewed apples. Bake in oven for 30 minutes at 190°C, 375°F, Gas Mark 5. Serve warm with cream or icecream.

Sheila Stiff
Lavenham

■ *For a spicy flavour, add cinnamon (1 tsp approx.) to dry ingredients, or sprinkle on the apples before covering with the topping.*

CHOCOLATE FUDGE PUDDING

Serves 4–6

75 g (3 oz) self-raising flour
2 tbsp cocoa
Pinch of salt
115 g (4 oz) margarine
115 g (4 oz) caster sugar
2 eggs
½ tsp vanilla essence
1–2 tbsp milk

Sauce
60–75 g (2–3 oz) soft brown sugar
2 tbsp cocoa
300 ml (½ pt) hot water

Cream margarine and sugar until pale and fluffy. Beat in the eggs. Fold in the sieved flour, cocoa and salt, and then the vanilla essence and milk. Spoon into a 1 ltr (2 pts) baking dish and spread evenly. The mixture should only half fill the dish.

Sauce: In a bowl combine the sugar and cocoa and stir in the hot water.

Pour over the cake mixture. Cook at 190°C, 375°F, Gas Mark 5, for 40 minutes. Serve at once.

Margaret Beverly
Lavenham

BANANA CREME BRULEE

This dessert is quick and easy, and tastes great.
For 4–6 servings you would need to reduce the ingredients accordingly.

450 g (1 lb) bananas, made into a
   paste
1.2 ltrs (2 pts) milk
1.2 ltrs (2 pts) whipping cream
1 vanilla pod
450 g (1 lb) sugar
15 eggs

Put milk, cream and vanilla pod into a saucepan and bring to the boil. In a separate bowl mix the eggs and sugar together into a light sabayon. When the milk has boiled, add to the egg mixture and whisk together. Add the banana paste to flavour and bake in ramekins at 180°C, 350°F, Gas Mark 4, for about 30 minutes.

Jason Buck, Head Chef
The Swan, Lavenham

CHOCOLATE TRUFFLE FANTASY

145 g (5 oz) almond macaroons,
   finely crushed
450 g (1 lb) plain chocolate
450 g (1 lb) marshmallows
   (mini-size best)
5 tbsp brandy (or half brandy with
   half sherry)
570 ml (1 pt) double cream
Cocoa powder for dusting

Line a 9 inch spring release cake tin with tin foil. Sprinkle crushed macaroons over base of tin. Break up chocolate and place in heatproof basin. Place marshmallows and brandy in another heatproof basin. Set basins over 2 pans of gently simmering water until dissolved, stirring frequently. Leave to cool for 5 minutes.

Meanwhile, whip cream until floppy. Fold half the cream into chocolate mixture. Gently fold in marshmallow mixture. Gradually add remaining cream and fold in until all blended.

Pour into a prepared tin. Cover with cling film, chill overnight. To serve turn onto a chilled plate and lightly dust with cocoa powder.

Jill Chrystal
Lavenham

BUTTERSCOTCH PUDDING

This is a wonderful winter's pudding for a cold winter's day.
Serve it hot with lots of cream or ice cream.
Serves 4

170 g (6 oz) soft brown sugar
85 g (3 oz) butter
115 g (4 oz) self-raising flour
2 eggs, beaten
1 tsp vanilla essence

Melt the sugar and butter in a saucepan. Stir in the flour and then the beaten eggs and vanilla essence.

Cook for 1 minute in the saucepan then pour into a well greased 6 inch (15 cm) tin.

Cook in oven for about 20–25 minutes at 180°C, 350°F, Gas Mark 4, until golden brown.

Bernadette Fraser and Ann Brewer
Authors of the Barn House Aga
Cookbook

RUMMY BANANAS

This dish is so easy and so tasty and always goes down well.
Serve it piping hot with cream.
Serves 4

4 large bananas, not too ripe
115 g (4 oz) butter
2 tbsp of dark rum or brandy
55 g (2 oz) muscovado sugar

Melt the butter in a frying pan. Add the peeled bananas and fry for 3–5 minutes until they begin to soften. Add the sugar and rum and cook until liquid bubbles. Divide into 4 portions and serve at once.

Evelyn Curtis
Lavenham

KIRSCH CREAM ICE
WITH COMPOTE OF BERRIES

Kirsch cream ice
600 ml (1 pt) cream
1 pkt of 6 meringue nests
3–4 tots Kirsch

Compote of berries
450 g (1 lb) strawberries
225 g (8 oz) raspberries
225 g (8 oz) blackberries
225 g (8 oz) blueberries
285 g (10 oz) cherries, stoned
  (in season)
1.2 ltrs (2 pts) water
225 g (8 oz) sugar
10 mint leaves
15 g (½ oz) icing sugar in a muslin
  bag

Pick over the fruit, remove stalks and wash. Keep back 1 x strawberry and 1 x blackberry per portion for garnish.

Bring water and sugar to the boil, making a stock syrup. Place the cherries into the simmering syrup, cover with a lid and bring back to the boil.

On the point of boiling, remove the cherries with a slotted spoon and place them into a glass bowl with a very small amount of syrup.

Repeat the process with the same stock syrup for each of the fruits in turn, using the lightest coloured fruit first. Cover the fruit and chill in fridge. Chill the remaining stock syrup.

Whisk the cream to the stiff peak stage. Lightly whisk in the Kirsch.

Break the meringues, *do not crush*, and carefully fold into the cream mixture.

Line a long tin or mould with clingfilm (for example a bread tin). Put the mixture into the tin to about 2 inch depth. Cover with clingfilm and freeze overnight.

Decorate plates with a single halved strawberry, a blackberry and a mint leaf. Make a small pile of mixed fruit compote on each plate.

Turn out the Kirsch cream, remove clingfilm. Cut into ½ inch slices with a hot knife and arrange around the fruit. Dust with a little icing sugar from a very fine muslin bag.

Janet Gillies
Lavenham

Notes
a) More Kirsch may be added to taste.
b) Do not add extra water unless absolutely necessary when poaching fruit.
c) Do not boil the fruit as it will break up.
d) A little of the chilled stock syrup may be used to flood the plate to aid presentation.
e) Meringue should be left quite large when adding it to the cream mix.

YOGHURT ICECREAM

A wonderful standby to keep in the freezer.
Serves 4

150 ml (¼ pt) preserve of your
  choice
150 ml (¼ pt) double cream
425 ml (¾ pt) natural yoghurt

Mix together and put into a plastic container and freeze. No need to take out and stir.
Jo Clerk, Lavenham

BLACKCURRANT CHEESECAKE

Makes one 9 inch cake

Base

75 g (3 oz) plus 1 tsp melted butter
175 g (6 oz) digestive biscuits,
* crushed*
2 tbsp sugar

Filling

700 g (1½ lb) full fat cream cheese
75 g (3 oz) caster sugar
3 eggs, separated
1 tsp grated lemon rind
1 tbsp cornflour mixed with 2 tbsp
* lemon juice*
125 g (4 oz) frozen blackcurrants
150 ml (5 fl oz) sour cream
2 tsp caster sugar
½ tsp vanilla essence

Pre-heat oven to 180°C, 350°F, Gas Mark 4. With the tsp of melted butter grease a 9 inch loose bottomed cake tin. In a medium sized mixing bowl combine the crushed digestive biscuits, sugar and remaining butter with wooden spoon. Spoon mixture into the cake tin and press it firmly, covering the bottom of the tin. In a large mixing bowl combine the cream cheese and sugar with a wooden spoon. Add the egg yolks and beat until smooth. Stir in the lemon rind/cornflour mixture and blackcurrants.

In another large mixing bowl beat the egg whites until they form stiff peaks. Fold the egg whites into the cheese mixture. Spoon the mixture into the prepared tin. Bake in the centre of the oven for 20 minutes or until the centre is firm when pressed with a finger tip. Remove the cake from oven and set aside to cool.

In a small bowl combine the sour cream, caster sugar and vanilla essence. Using a palette knife, spread the sour cream mixture over top of cake.

When completely cool take from tin and chill it in refrigerator before serving. Enjoy!

This blackcurrant cheesecake is a speciality of Strattons Hotel, in Norfolk, and was featured in the May 1997 edition of *Homes and Gardens*. The owners of this hotel, Les and Vanessa Scott, have very kindly given me this recipe for the Lavenham Church Cookbook

Cakes and Bakes

Lady Redesdale's Bread 44

Jiffy Cake 44

Light Mincemeat Streusel
Cake 44

Suffolk Rusks 45

Granny Sykes' Parkin 45

Walnut Soda Bread 45

Lime Meringue Roulade 46

My Mother's Oatcakes 46

Foolproof All-in-One
Chocolate Cake 47

Corncraft Almond Slice 47

All Things Nice Cake 47

Apple and Walnut Cake 48

Lemon Dessert Cake 48

Melting Moments 48

Orange and Walnut Cake 49

Chocolate Crispies 49

Paradise Squares 49

Chocolate Orange Drizzle
Cake 50

Quick Ginger Biscuits 50

Chocolate and Brandy or
Whisky Cake 50

Tea Loaf 51

Barn House Breakfast
Bread 51

Lemon Cake 51

Date Fingers 52

Basic Semi-Rich Cake 52

Easter Biscuits 52

Chocolate Traybake 53

One-stage Cheese Scones 53

Chocolate, Cherry and
Nut Cake 54

Christmas Festive Cake 54

White Christmas Cake 54

Low-fat Moist Carrot Cake ... 55

One-stage Fruity
Rock Buns 56

Belgian Marmalade
Slices 56

Carrot Cake 57

Fifteens 58

LADY REDESDALE'S BREAD

225 g (8 oz) strong white flour
700 g (1½ lb) wholemeal flour
3 tsp salt

Put above in a mixing bowl. Make a well in centre of the flour and put in 25 g (1 oz) fresh yeast, 6 tsp sugar and 300 ml (½ pt) luke warm water. Leave for 10 minutes until yeast has "fuzzed" up. Add another 300 ml (½ pt) warm water. Mix to a good dough and knead for 5 minutes. Leave to rise in a warm place for 1 hour. Cut into 2 loaves and let rise for half an hour in baking tins. Bake for half an hour at 200°C, 400°F, Gas Mark 6.

The Duchess of Devonshire
Chatsworth, Bakewell, Derby

JIFFY CAKE

175 g (6 oz) quick creaming
   margarine
175 g (6 oz) caster sugar
2 eggs
225 g (8 oz) self-raising flour
1 level tsp baking powder
4 tbsp milk, fruit juice or cider

Put all the ingredients into a large mixing bowl, then beat for several minutes. Put into a well greased and floured 7 inch sandwich tin and bake for approximately 1 hour, 180°C, 350°F, Gas Mark 4.

The cake may be iced, or cut in half and filled with jam and cream.

Joan Lawrence Veasey
Lavenham

LIGHT MINCEMEAT STREUSEL CAKE

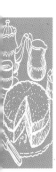

Almond topping
40 g (1½ oz) butter, melted
50 g (2 oz) plain flour or soya flour
25 g (1 oz) light soft brown sugar
50 g (2 oz) flaked almonds

Cake
115 g (4 oz) butter, softened
115 g (4 oz) caster sugar
Grated zest of orange and lemon
2 medium eggs, beaten
225 g (8 oz) self-raising flour
411 g jar mincemeat
1 tbsp brandy or fruit juice

Pre-heat oven to 170°C, 325°F, Gas Mark 3. Grease and line 8 x 3½ inch deep loose base tin. Make topping by rubbing in butter and flour. Stir in sugar and almonds. Set aside.

Cake: Cream butter and sugar with zests until pale and fluffy. Gradually add eggs alternating with flour. Fold in mincemeat. Add brandy until mixture drops easily from spoon. Turn mixture into cake tin, level top and scatter topping evenly over cake mixture.

Bake on centre shelf for approximately 1¾ hours. Test. Cool for 15 minutes in tin before turning out. Store for one week in airtight container. Dust with icing sugar.

Anon

SUFFOLK RUSKS

225 g (8 oz) self-raising flour
Pinch of salt
75 g (3 oz) butter
1 egg
Milk or water to mix

Sift flour and salt together. Rub in the butter lightly and mix with beaten egg and just enough milk or water to make a smooth dough.

Roll out lightly, 1 inch thick, and cut into 2½ inch rounds. Place on a baking sheet and cook at 230°C, 450°F, Gas Mark 8, for 10 minutes.

Remove from oven and split in half by hand. Replace on baking sheet with cut sides upward.

Bake at 190°C, 375°F, Gas Mark 5, for 10–15 minutes until crisp and golden. Cool, and serve with butter and cheese or jam.

These rusks store well in a tin.

Diana Anscombe
Lavenham

GRANNY SYKES' PARKIN

350 g (12 oz) medium cut oatmeal
75 g (3 oz) plain flour
250 g (9 oz) soft light brown sugar
250 g (9 oz) treacle
115 g (4 oz) margarine
15 g (½ oz) lard
2 tsp baking powder
1 tsp ginger
2 eggs
1 tbsp milk
Pinch of salt

Grease and line a large roasting tin. Cream margarine, lard and sugar, then add treacle, eggs, flour, baking powder and ginger. Mix well with salt, oatmeal and milk.

Bake slowly for approximately 1 hour 40 minutes at 140°C, 275°F, Gas Mark 1. Cool and cut into squares.

Vickie Weaver
Lavenham

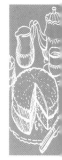

WALNUT SODA BREAD

400 g (14 oz) high extraction flour
  – ie Marriages, Jordans or
  similar
2 tsp bicarbonate of soda
2 tsp cream of tartar
1 tsp fine salt
50 g (2 oz) rolled oats
75 g (3 oz) chopped walnuts
150 ml (5 fl oz) milk mixed with
  150 ml (5 fl oz) natural yoghurt

Mix all dry ingredients together in a large bowl.

Add milk and yoghurt mixture and draw together, kneading in the bowl until dough is just firm and slightly sticky.

Form into a ball, place on a greased baking sheet and cut a cross on top with a sharp knife and bake in a pre-heated oven at 190°C, 375°F, Gas Mark 5, for about 40 minutes until loaf sounds hollow when tapped on the bottom.

Cool on wire rack. Excellent with unsalted butter and honey.

Maureen Allen
Lavenham

LIME MERINGUE ROULADE

A meringue roulade is quicker and easier to do than a lemon meringue pie and is just as popular.

Makes 8–10 slices

5 egg whites
275 g (10 oz) caster sugar
50 g (2 oz) flaked almonds

Filling
300 ml (½ pt) double cream
Grated rind and juice of 1 small
 lime
2 tbsp good lemon or lime curd

Pre-heat oven to 220°C, 425°F, Gas Mark 7. Line a 13 x 9 inch (33 x 23 cm) Swiss roll tin with greased non-stick paper or greased lift off.

Whisk the egg whites in an electric mixer on full speed until very stiff. Gradually add the sugar, a tsp at a time, and still on high speed, whisking well between each addition. Whisk until very, very stiff and all the sugar has been added.

Spread the meringue mixture into the prepared tin and sprinkle with the almonds. Place the tin in the pre-heated oven and bake for about 8 minutes until very golden. Then lower the temperature to 160°C, 325°F, Gas Mark 3, and bake the roulade for a further 15 minutes until firm to the touch.

Remove the meringue from the oven and turn almond side down on to a sheet of non-stick baking paper. Remove the paper from the base of the cooked meringue and allow to cool for about 10 minutes.

Lightly whip the cream, add lime rind and juice and fold in the lemon curd. Spread evenly over the meringue. Roll up the meringue fairly tightly from the long end to form a roulade. Wrap in non-stick baking paper and chill well before serving. Serve with raspberries if liked.

This recipe was kindly sent to me by Mary Berry, well-known for the many cookery books she has written, and for her numerous television appearances

MY MOTHER'S OATCAKES

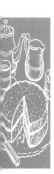

175 g (6 oz) porridge oats
35 g (1½ oz) Trex
50 g (2 oz) butter
50 g (2 oz) caster sugar
Pinch of salt

Put all ingredients into a bowl and knead to a pliable state. Press into greased patty tins and level off.

Bake for about 30 minutes at 160–170°C, 325°F, Gas Mark 3. Leave in tin until cool.

They taste even better if kept for several days.

**Marguerite Hayward
Lavenham**

■ *A trial and error recipe, which reminds me of my Mother's oatcakes. My young sons soon became addicted, and when we later visited the elder one, who was at college in America, he demanded oatcakes! The Customs Officer looked at the tin and asked the contents – "Oatcakes" – he opened it up and said "Ah, cookies, they look good". But he didn't get one!*

FOOLPROOF ALL-IN-ONE CHOCOLATE CAKE

150 g (5 oz) self-raising flour
25 g (1 oz) cocoa
175 g (6 oz) soft margarine
3 large eggs
175 g (6 oz) caster sugar
1 tbsp golden syrup
2 tbsp milk

Filling
50 g (2 oz) butter
115 g (4 oz) sifted icing sugar
1 tsp instant coffee granules

Grease and line a 7 inch round cake tin. Put the margarine, eggs, caster sugar, sifted flour and cocoa powder, golden syrup and milk into a mixing bowl (or a food processor) and mix together, then beat until well incorporated. Turn the mixture into the tin, hollow out the centre slightly.

Bake on centre shelf of oven at 180°C, 350°F, Gas Mark 4 (160°C for fan ovens), for approximately 1½ hours, or until a warm skewer pushed into the centre of the cake comes out clean. Turn the cake onto a wire tray to cool.

To make filling, beat the butter and icing sugar together. Add the coffee granules diluted with a small amount of hot water. Split the cake and sandwich together with the coffee cream.

Jo Wright
Lavenham

CORNCRAFT ALMOND SLICE

175 g (6 oz) shortcrust pastry
115 g (4 oz) caster sugar
175 g (6 oz) ground almonds
115 g (4 oz) icing sugar

Roll pastry to fit a Swiss roll tin. Mix the rest of the ingredients with 2 eggs beaten with a tsp of almond essence. Cover top with almond flakes and glace cherries. Bake for 25 minutes at 160–170°C, 325°F, Gas Mark 3.

The Corncraft
Monks Eleigh
Suffolk

ALL THINGS NICE CAKE

115 g (4 oz) butter or margarine
60 g (2 oz) coconut
115 g (4 oz) caster sugar
175 g (6 oz) self-raising flour
2 eggs
2 tbsp milk

Beat sugar and butter to a creamy consistency. Add eggs slowly with a little flour. Beat well. Fold in flour and coconut. Pour into a 7 inch square tin, greased and lined. Bake for about 1 hour at 160–170°C, 325°F, Gas Mark 3. Split in half when cold and fill with this mixture. 175 g (6 oz) icing sugar, sifted, 75 g (3 oz) butter, 1 dsp milk and 1 tsp cinnamon. Beat these ingredients together until smooth.

Mary Holland
Lavenham

APPLE AND WALNUT CAKE

A quick and easy to make traditional cake – a slice of this cake goes well with some Wensleydale cheese.

225 g (8 oz) plain flour
1 tsp baking powder
2 tsp mixed spice
100 g (4 oz) butter
175 g (6 oz) soft dark brown sugar
3 medium eggs
115 g (4 oz) sultanas
115 g (4 oz) walnuts, chopped
225 g (8 oz) peeled apples, diced

Grease and line an 8 inch deep cake tin. Sift flour, baking powder and spice into a bowl. Rub butter into flour until mixture resembles fine breadcrumbs. Stir in remaining ingredients, mix well and place in tin. Cook for 1¼ hours until dark golden and springy to the touch at 180°C, 350°F, Gas Mark 4 (fan oven 150°C, middle shelf 1¼ hours). Leave to stand in tin for 30 minutes before turning out.

Evelyn Curtis, Lavenham

LEMON DESSERT CAKE

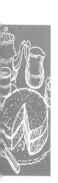

3 eggs separated
150 g (5 oz) caster sugar
1½ lemons, rind and juice
60 g (2½ oz) cornflour
275 ml (½ pt) double cream
225 g (8 oz) homemade lemon
  curd

Use an 8 inch spring release cake tin, oiled and dusted with caster sugar and cornflour.

Beat egg yolks with caster sugar and rind of lemon until light in colour and creamy. Gradually add lemon juice and beat until mixture leaves a trail. Fold in cornflour. Whisk egg whites until stiff, fold into lemon mixture. Spoon into tin, and bake for 40 minutes at 180°C, 350°F, Gas Mark 4. Leave to cool in tin for at least 5 minutes before turning out. Serve with lemon cream – whisk cream until floppy, gradually spoon in lemon curd, whisk after each addition to blend.

Jill Chrystal
Lavenham

MELTING MOMENTS

These are good coffee morning biscuits.

50 g (2 oz) margarine
40 g (1½ oz) caster sugar
¼ of a beaten egg
Few drops of vanilla essence
60 g (2½ oz) self-raising flour
Rolled oats
A few glace cherries

Lightly grease a baking tray. Cream the margarine and sugar together. Add the beaten egg and vanilla essence. Fold in flour. Form into a stiff dough, divide into 10 portions. Form each piece into a ball and roll in the rolled oats and place on baking tray. Top each with a piece of cherry. Bake for 15–20 minutes at 190°C, 375°F, Gas Mark 5.

Renée Attew
Lavenham

ORANGE AND WALNUT CAKE

225 g (8 oz) self-raising flour
¼ tsp salt
175 g (6 oz) butter
175 g (6 oz) caster sugar
3 large eggs
Rind of 1 orange
25 g (1 oz) chopped mixed peel
50 g (2 oz) walnuts, chopped
1 tbsp of concentrated orange
  juice

Icing
225 g (8 oz) icing sugar
2–3 tbsp concentrated orange
  juice

Sift flour and salt together. Cream butter and sugar and add beaten eggs. Add half the flour and other ingredients and blend. Add the rest of the flour.

Spoon the mixture into a 7 inch greased and lined cake tin and cook in a pre-heated oven 180°C, 350°F, Gas Mark 4 for 1¼ hours. (For Aga owners use the cake-bake on the floor of the top oven).

For the icing: Warm icing sugar and concentrated orange juice together in a pan until smooth. Ice the cake with this mixture while icing is still warm. Be careful not to overheat the icing when blending.

Janet Ellis
Lavenham

■ *This recipe was taken from a Celebrity Recipe Book in aid of the Leonard Cheshire Homes and was donated to the book by Mrs Margaret Thatcher. I have tried and tested this – it is delicious, but I add 1 tsp of baking powder to the self-raising flour before sifting.*

CHOCOLATE CRISPIES

60 g (2 oz) butter
2 tbsp Golden syrup
60 g (2 oz) icing sugar
2 level tbsp cocoa

Melt the above ingredients in a large pan. Take pan off the heat and add 1 cup of sultanas and 75 g (3 oz) cornflakes. Stir well, covering the cornflakes with the chocolate mixture. Put into baking cases and allow to cool.

Sue Crighton, Lavenham

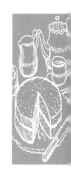

PARADISE SQUARES

170 g (6 oz) short crust pastry to
  line Swiss roll tin
115 g (4 oz) margarine
115 g (4 oz) caster sugar
60 g (2 oz) ground rice
60 g (2 oz) chopped walnuts
60 g (2 oz) glace cherries
1 egg

Cream margarine and sugar, then beat egg and add to the mixture. Mix in ground rice, nuts and fruit and spread mixture over the pastry case. Smooth top and bake at 200°C, 400°F, Gas Mark 6, for 30–35 minutes until golden brown. Remove from oven and while still warm, sprinkle with granulated sugar. Cut into squares when cool.

Eileen Huffey
Lavenham

CHOCOLATE ORANGE DRIZZLE CAKE

175 g (6 oz) margarine
175 g (6 oz) caster sugar
3 eggs
175 g (6 oz) self-raising flour
2 tbsp milk
Finely grated rind of 2 oranges

Orange syrup
Juice of 2 oranges
110 g (4 oz) caster sugar

Topping
110 g (4 oz) good chocolate,
    melted with 10 g (½ oz) butter

Line 2 lb tin with foil. Cream margarine and sugar until soft. Beat eggs, one at a time, into mixture. Fold in sifted flour and slowly add milk. Add finely grated rind of oranges. Cook 180°C, 350°F, Gas Mark 4, for 1 hour. When nearly cool make slits across top of cake with a sharp knife and drizzle on orange syrup. When cold top with chocolate topping.

Pat Dilliway
Lavenham

QUICK GINGER BISCUITS

175 g (6 oz) plain flour
100 g (3½ oz) caster sugar
75 g (3 oz) margarine
1 tbsp treacle
2 level tsp ground ginger
1 level tsp salt
1 egg to bind

Rub fat into flour. Add dry ingredients and mix stiffly with egg and treacle. Roll out thinly, cut into shapes and bake on flat tin for 15 minutes at 190°C, 375°F, Gas Mark 5.

Kit Featherstone
Lavenham

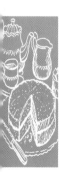

CHOCOLATE AND BRANDY OR WHISKY CAKE

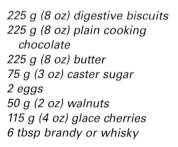

225 g (8 oz) digestive biscuits
225 g (8 oz) plain cooking
    chocolate
225 g (8 oz) butter
75 g (3 oz) caster sugar
2 eggs
50 g (2 oz) walnuts
115 g (4 oz) glace cherries
6 tbsp brandy or whisky

Melt butter and chocolate. Crush biscuits coarsely. Chop cherries into small pieces. Chop walnuts. Mix these ingredients together with melted butter and chocolate. Beat eggs and sugar until creamy, add this to mixture. Lastly, add brandy or whisky.

Grease a 2 lb loaf tin with butter. Pour ingredients into tin and place in fridge for 8 hours or longer if necessary. To remove from tin, run a flat knife around edge. Stand in hot water for a few minutes then turn upside down onto a flat plate and cut into slices.

Decorate to your own choice with chopped fruit. Without the decoration it will freeze well.

Eva Fear
Paulton, Somerset

TEA LOAF

450 g (1 lb) mixed fruit
1 breakfast cup of soft brown
   sugar
1 breakfast cup of cold tea

Put into a bowl, cover and leave overnight to soak in fridge. Then add 1 large beaten egg, 2 breakfast cups of self-raising flour and beat together. Place in a greased loaf tin (1 large or 2 small tins) Cook 160–170°C, 325°F. Gas Mark 3, for 1–2 hours, depending on size of tin.

Sue Crighton
Lavenham

BARN HOUSE BREAKFAST BREAD

If you would rather have this wonderfully easy to make bread with cooked meats and cheese for lunch, replace the muesli with a handful of chopped olives, nuts and sliced sun-dried tomatoes.

455 g (1 lb) self-raising flour
115 g (4 oz) muesli
60 ml (2 fl oz) vegetable oil
1 egg, beaten
Milk to bind

Mix flour and muesli together. Add the egg, oil and enough milk to make a firm dough.

Shape into a round, flatten to 2 inches (5 cm) thick and place on a floured baking tray. Sprinkle with flour.

Bake at 180°C, 350°F, Gas Mark 4, for about 35 minutes – until it sounds hollow when tapped.

Note for Aga owners: *Two Oven Aga* – Place on the grid shelf on the bottom set of runners in the roasting oven with the cold shelf in the middle of the oven for about 35 minutes, until it sounds hollow when tapped.

Four Oven Aga – Place on the grid shelf on the second set of runners in the baking oven for about 35 minutes, until it sounds hollow when tapped.

Bernadette Fraser and Ann Brewer
Authors of the Barn House Aga
Cookbook

LEMON CAKE

250 g (9 oz) soft margarine
250 g (9 oz) caster sugar
4 whole eggs
250 g (9 oz) sifted plain flour
2 tsp baking powder

Sauce
125 g (4½ oz) caster sugar, juice and grated rind of 2 oranges and 1 lemon.

Stir and leave in a warm place, stirring occasionally to dissolve the sugar.

Mix and beat all the ingredients together, adding the eggs one at a time between each beating.

Bake in a 9 inch loose bottomed cake tin at 150°C, 300°F, Gas Mark 2, for 1¼ hours.

Turn out onto a plate. Prick cake with skewer and pour lemon and orange juice over the still hot cake.

Maureen Allen
Lavenham

DATE FINGERS

75 g (3 oz) self-raising flour
25 g (1 oz) butter
75 g (3 oz) caster sugar
1 medium egg
115 g (4 oz) dates
50 g (2 oz) walnuts
2 tbsp homemade wine or sherry
Icing sugar

Chop the dates and walnuts. Melt the butter in a saucepan, beat the egg and add it and the sugar to the melted butter. Next, add the wine or sherry, the chopped dates, walnuts and flour.

Stir well and spread in a greased Swiss roll tin. Bake for 15–20 minutes at 180°C, 350°F, Gas Mark 4. Leave to cool in tin.

Dredge with icing sugar and cut into fingers.

Evelyn Curtis
Lavenham

BASIC SEMI-RICH CAKE

175 g (6 oz) soft margarine
175 g (6 oz) caster or brown sugar
3 medium eggs
115 g (4 oz) self-raising flour
115 g (4 oz) plain flour
225 g (8 oz) mixed dried fruit or a
    few vanilla drops and 75 g (3 oz)
    walnuts
Pinch of salt

Cream together fat and sugar. Add eggs, beating between each addition. Fold in flour, fruit or vanilla and walnuts. Bake in a greased and lined 7 inch cake tin for 1¾ hours at 150°C, 300°F, Gas Mark 2. Cool in tin for 5 minutes before turning out on wire rack.

Kit Featherstone, Lavenham

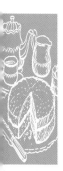

EASTER BISCUITS

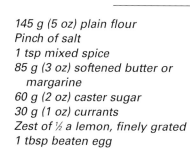

145 g (5 oz) plain flour
Pinch of salt
1 tsp mixed spice
85 g (3 oz) softened butter or
    margarine
60 g (2 oz) caster sugar
30 g (1 oz) currants
Zest of ½ a lemon, finely grated
1 tbsp beaten egg

Sift flour, salt and mixed spice onto a plate. In a bowl cream together the butter and sugar, then add flour mixture, currants, lemon zest and egg. Mix to a smooth dough. On a floured surface roll out to about ¼ inch (5 mm) thick and cut into rounds with a 2 inch (5 cm) cutter.

Place biscuits on a greased baking sheet and bake at 180°C, 350°F, Gas Mark 4, for 15–20 minutes until golden brown.

Note for Aga owners: *Two Oven Aga* – Place in the roasting oven on the grid shelf on the bottom set of runners with the cold shelf in the middle for about 15 minutes.

Four Oven Aga – Place in the baking oven on the grid shelf on the second set of runners for about 20 minutes.

Bernadette Fraser and Ann Brewer
Authors of the Barn House Aga
Cookbook

CHOCOLATE TRAYBAKE

A really good recipe, perfect for large families,
coffee mornings, bazaars and school fetes.

45 g (1½ oz) cocoa, sieved
4 tbsp boiling water
175 g (6 oz) soft margarine
225 g (8 oz) self-raising flour and
  1½ level tsp baking powder,
  sieved together
175 g (6 oz) caster sugar
3 eggs
About 3 tbsp milk

Chocolate icing
60 g (2 oz) margarine
45 g (1½ oz) cocoa, sieved
225 g (8 oz) icing sugar, sieved
About 2 tbsp milk
4 good tbsp apricot jam, warmed

Heat the oven to 180°C, 350°F, Gas Mark 4. Take a roasting tin about 12 x 8½ inches (30 x 21 cm). Line base with a piece of greased greaseproof or greased foil before adding the cake mixture.

Measure cocoa into a large roomy bowl. Blend with boiling water until smooth, add all the ingredients, beat well for about 2 minutes until well blended.

Turn the mixture into the tin and smooth the top. Bake in oven for about 35–40 minutes, until the cake has shrunk from the sides of the tin and springs back when pressed in the centre with the fingertips.

Leave to cool in the tin and spread with warmed apricot jam.

For the chocolate icing: Melt the margarine gently in a pan, add cocoa and stir well for 1 minute and remove from the heat.

Stir in the icing sugar and milk and mix until smooth. Cool until a coating consistency, then pour over the cake.

Spread evenly. Allow to set and decorate with Maltesers. Cut into about 21 pieces.

This recipe was kindly sent to me by Mary Berry, well-known for the many cookery books she has written, and for her numerous television appearances

ONE-STAGE CHEESE SCONES

These make a quick tea-time favourite.

50 g (2 oz) luxury margarine
225 g (8 oz) self-raising flour,
  1 rounded tsp baking power,
  ¼ level tsp salt, ½ level tsp dry
  mustard, sieved together
75 g (3 oz) Cheddar cheese, finely
  grated
5 tbsp milk
1 small egg
Milk to glaze

Put all the ingredients into a mixing bowl.

Mix thoroughly to form a scone dough. Turn onto a lightly floured surface.

Roll out to ½ inch thickness.

Cut into rounds with a 2 inch cutter.

Brush the tops with milk.

Put onto a baking sheet and bake for 12–15 minutes, 220°C, 425°F, Gas Mark 7.

Renée Attew
Lavenham

CHOCOLATE, CHERRY AND NUT CAKE

115 g (4 oz) self-raising flour
1 level tsp baking powder
115 g (4 oz) soft margarine
85 g (3 oz) caster sugar
2 eggs
30 g (1 oz) plain chocolate, grated
85 g (3 oz) glace cherries,
    chopped
15 g (½ oz) walnuts, chopped

Sift flour and baking powder into a bowl. Add other ingredients and mix well, then beat for 2 minutes. Put mixture evenly into a 450 g (1 lb) loaf tin and bake in the centre of the oven for 50–60 minutes at 170°C, 325°F, Gas Mark 3.

Eileen Huffey
Lavenham

CHRISTMAS FESTIVE CAKE

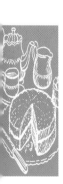

1½ cups whole brazil nuts
1½ cups walnut halves
225 g (½ lb) stoned dates
⅔ cup chopped candied peel
½ cup red whole maraschino cherries
½ cup green whole maraschino
    cherries
½ cup seeded raisins
¾ cup plain flour
½ tsp baking powder
½ tsp salt
¾ cup caster sugar
3 eggs
1 tsp vanilla essence
Rum to taste

Grease an 8 inch tin and line with greaseproof paper. Place fruit and nuts in a basin and pour over rum. Sift flour, baking powder and salt 2 or 3 times, then mix with sugar.

Add to fruit and nuts and mix well. Make into mixture with beaten eggs and vanilla essence.

Spoon into tin and press down with back of spoon. Bake in a slow oven for 2–2½ hours. Leave in tin for 10 minutes then turn onto rack until cold.

Keep in a plastic bag in fridge – it will keep for months. Serve in small slices.

Mrs Marjorie Jones and Anne
Lavenham

WHITE CHRISTMAS CAKE

285 g (10 oz) butter or margarine
285 g (10 oz) caster sugar
285 g (10 oz) plain flour, sieved
    with 1 tsp baking power
4 eggs
170 g (6 oz) ground almonds
60 g (2 oz) glace pineapple,
    chopped
60 g (2 oz) glace ginger, chopped
115 g (4 oz) glace cherries,
    chopped

Beat sugar and butter together, add eggs, beating well. Then add flour and ground almonds and mix well.

Add chopped pineapple, ginger and glace cherries to the mixture. Line and grease a 9 inch cake tin and bake at 150°C, 300°F, Gas Mark 2, for 1½– 2 hours.

Margaret Garside
Lavenham

LOW-FAT MOIST CARROT CAKE

*I have been making carrot cake for years, and each time it seems
to improve with a little tinkering here and there. Last year I attempted
a low-fat version rather reluctantly, not believing it was possible.
Now I have to admit it's become one of my favourites.
It's also one of the quickest, easiest cakes ever.*

Serves 12

*175 g (6 oz) dark brown soft sugar,
   sifted*
2 large eggs at room temperature
120 ml (4 fl oz) sunflower oil
*200 g (7 oz) wholemeal self-raising
   flour*
1½ tsp bicarbonate of soda
3 rounded tsp mixed spice
Grated zest of 1 orange
*200 g (7 oz) carrots, peeled and
   coarsely grated*
175 g (6 oz) sultanas

Topping
*250 g (9 oz) Quark (skimmed milk
   soft cheese)*
20 g (¾ oz) caster sugar
2 tsp vanilla extract
*1 rounded tsp ground cinnamon,
   plus a little extra for dusting*

Syrup glaze
Juice ½ small orange
1 dsp lemon juice
40 g (1½ oz) dark brown sugar

You will need a non-stick baking tin measuring 10 x 6 inches (25½ x 15 cm) and 1 inch (2.5 cm) deep, the base lined with silicone paper (parchment).

Pre-heat oven to 170°C, 325°F, Gas Mark 3.

Begin by whisking the sugar, eggs and oil together in a bowl using an electric hand whisk for 2–3 minutes.

Then sift together the flour, bicarbonate of soda and the mixed spice into the bowl, tipping in all the bits of bran that are left in the sieve.

Now stir all this together, then fold in the orange zest, carrots and sultanas. After that pour the mixture into the prepared tin and bake on the centre shelf of the oven for 35–40 minutes, until it is well risen and feels firm and springy to the touch when lightly pressed in the centre.

While the cake is cooking, make the topping by mixing all the ingredients in a bowl until light and fluffy, then cover with clingfilm and chill for 1–2 hours or until needed.

Now you need to make the syrup glaze, and to do this whisk together the fruit juices and sugar in a bowl.

Then, when the cake comes out of the oven, stab it all over with a skewer and quickly spoon the syrup over as evenly as possible.

Now leave the cake on one side to cool in the tin, during which time the syrup will be absorbed.

When the cake is completely cold, remove it from the tin, spread the topping over, cut it into 12 squares and dust with a little cinnamon.

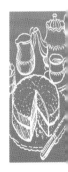

**© Delia Smith 1998 – Recipe
reproduced by permission from
Delia's How to Cook (published
by BBC Worldwide Ltd.)**

ONE-STAGE FRUITY ROCK BUNS

Makes approximately 10–12

225g (8 oz) self-raising flour
½ level tsp baking powder
115 g (4 oz) Blue Band margarine
75 g (3 oz) caster sugar
115 g (4 oz) mixed dried fruit and
peel
1 standard egg
1 tbsp milk

Place all ingredients in a mixing bowl and beat together for 2–3 minutes.

Place heaped tsp of the mixture well apart on baking sheets, previously brushed with oil or melted margarine.

Bake in pre-heated oven 200°C, 400°F, Gas Mark 6, on second and third shelves from top of oven for 15–20 minutes. Remove and cool on wire tray.

Evelyn Curtis, Lavenham

BELGIAN MARMALADE SLICES

A shortbread type of dough with an unusual textures. It is grated into the tin and given a tart marmalade and apricot centre.

Makes approximately 24

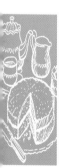

350 g (12 oz) butter or soft
margarine
150 g (5 oz) caster sugar
3 tbsp sunflower or vegetable oil
1 tsp vanilla essence
¼ tsp almond essence
1 large egg
1 egg yolk
675 g (1½ lb) plain flour
1 level tbsp baking powder

Filling

450 g (1 lb) coarse-cut mature
marmalade
176 g (6 oz) ready-to-eat apricots,
chopped
Grated rind of 1 lemon
2 tbsp lemon juice
40 g (1½ oz) slivered blanched
almonds
Little icing sugar for dredging

Cream the butter and sugar together until soft and creamy, then beat in the oil followed by the essences, egg and egg yolk. Sift together the flour and baking powder and gradually work into the mixture until evenly blended. Line a Swiss roll tin (approx. 30 x 23 cm) 12 x 9 inches with greased greaseproof paper or non-stick baking paper. Combine the marmalade, chopped apricots, lemon rind and juice. Take just under half the dough and press it out evenly to cover the tin. Spread evenly with the marmalade mixture. Using a coarse grater, grate the remaining dough a little at a time, and spoon it evenly over the fruit mixture. Sprinkle with the almonds and bake in a pre-heated oven at 150°C, 300°F, Gas Mark 2, for an hour. Remove from the oven and leave to cool in the tin. Wrap in cling film or foil and leave for 24 hours (this is important). Then dredge lightly with sifted icing sugar and serve cut into finger or squares. Store in an airtight container for up to 10 days, or freeze for up to 3 months.

This recipe was given to me by Rosemary Wadey to include in this book. Rosemary is well-known for the many cookery books she has written.

CARROT CAKE

I know, another carrot cake, but this is one with a difference. It doesn't have a cream topping, has nuts and raisins in it, and you can substitute the carrots with bananas to make a banana cake.

225 g (8 oz) butter
350 g (12 oz) soft light brown sugar
275 g (10 oz) plain flour
2 tsp baking powder
1 tsp cinnamon
1 tsp ground ginger
Pinch of ground nutmeg
4 eggs
225 g (8 oz) carrots, grated
175 g (6 oz) raisins
100 g (4 oz) chopped walnuts
½ tsp vanilla essence

Pre-heat oven to 180°C, 350°F, Gas Mark 4.

Beat butter and sugar until creamy. Sieve together flour, baking powder, cinnamon, ginger and nutmeg. Add one egg to the creamed mixture with a little sieved flour. Then mix in carrots and the other ingredients. Bake for 1¼–1½ hours.

Laraine Mann
Great Cornard

FIFTEENS

These little sweetmeats, or biscuits, are aptly named, as you will see from the following ingredients. I have found them to be most popular, whether served with coffee or tea. Small and attractive to the eye, they can even take their place on any special buffet table, and I guarantee they will disappear in minutes – so it's always advisable to keep a supply handy in your fridge. Incidentally, I find most guests ask what the ingredients are, and surprised when I tell them!

15 Digestive biscuits
15 Marshmallows (white & pink)
15 glace cherries
1 medium sized tin of
  unsweetened condensed milk
Sufficient quantity of desiccated
  coconut for "rolling"

Put the biscuits in a strong polythene bag and either crush the biscuits with a rolling pin or, as I do, be ruthless and give them a few hard stamps with your feet. Keeping biscuits in bag.

Cut the marshmallows into small pieces (I find having a jug of hot water and dipping in the blades of my kitchen scissors stops the marshmallows sticking together). Cut the glace cherries into quarters and mix all these ingredients together with the condensed milk – this is best done by hand.

Spread a sufficient quantity of desiccated coconut on a clean flat surface, and begin by rolling a quantity of the mixture into sausage shapes, usually about 8"–9" long, thoroughly coating with coconut. Wrap each sausage in tin foil and put into your fridge to chill and firm up. When you are ready to use them cut into one inch pieces, arrange and serve on one of your prettiest china plates, and remember to keep your guests guessing, unless they have bought this book, when your secret will be out!

Evelyn Curtis
Lavenham

Preserves

Strawberry Jam 60

Quick Raspberry Jam 60

Pecan and Almond Mincemeat 60

Lemon Curd 61

Tomato Marmalade 61

Runner Bean Chutney (Sweet) 61

Tomato Chutney 62

Autumn Fruit Chutney 62

Marrow and Apple Chutney 62

Military Pickles 63

STRAWBERRY JAM

Yield: 5 lb

1.5 kg (3½ lb) hulled strawberries
Juice of 1½ lemons
1.37 kg (3 lb) preserving sugar,
  granulated will do

Heat the strawberries and lemon juice gently in a pan, stirring constantly to reduce the volume.

Add sugar, stir until dissolved and boil until setting point is reached, about 20 minutes (test spoonful on a cold saucer, the surface should begin to wrinkle when it is pushed with a finger).

Remove scum from jam (a knob of butter will help disperse the scum and make jam glossy).

Leave jam undisturbed to cool until a skin forms on the surface and the fruit sinks (about 20 minutes).

Pour into warm, dry jars and cover immediately with waxed discs.

Tie down when cold.

Evelyn Curtis
Lavenham

QUICK RASPBERRY JAM

This is an old recipe – delicious, but does not keep as well as the traditional boiled raspberry jam.

For each 450 g (1 lb) of raspberries use 570 g (1¼ lb) sugar. Bring fruit to the boil and boil for not more than 2–3 minutes.

Add sugar and stir until quite dissolved. Bring again almost to

boiling point and put immediately into warmed pots, cover while hot; the flavour of the fresh fruit is thus retained.

Evelyn Curtis
Lavenham

PECAN AND ALMOND MINCEMEAT

60 g (2 oz) pecans
60 g (2 oz) almonds
60 g (2 oz) dried figs
340 g (12 oz) apples
255 g (9 oz) sultanas
170 g (6 oz) shredded suet
2 medium oranges
1 tsp cinnamon
1 tsp nutmeg
½ tsp allspice
115 g (4 oz) dark brown sugar
285 ml (10 fl oz) brandy

Mix all dry ingredients, then add strained juice of the 2 oranges and brandy, mixing well again.

Leave overnight, then stir again. Leave for 6 weeks!

Barbara Pearmain
Lavenham

LEMON CURD

Homemade Lemon curd is vastly superior to the commercial version. It can be varied by using limes – you'll need 5 to replace the 4 lemons, or use 2 lemons and 2 sweet oranges to make St. Clement's Curd (using the main recipe).

Makes about 675 g (1½ lb)

Grated rind and juice of 4 lemons
4 eggs
125 g (4 oz) butter
350 g (12 oz) caster sugar

Place all the ingredients in a large bowl or in the top of a double boiler. Blend together then sit on top of a pan of simmering water. Stir continuously until the sugar has dissolved and continue heating gently for about 20 minutes until the curd thickens; do not allow it to boil or it will curdle. Pour into small warm jars, cover, label and store in the fridge.

Celia Goodrick-Clarke
Cookery Writer, Daily Mail

■ *Use a jar of lemon curd to make a quick icecream, fold enough lemon curd into a bowl of whipped cream (or softened good quality vanilla icecream) to give a good flavour. Freeze in a plastic container in the usual way.*

TOMATO MARMALADE

Makes from 910 g–1.37 kg (2 lb–3 lb)

675 g (1½ lb) ripe tomatoes
2 small sweet oranges
1 large lemon
675 g (1½ lb) granulated sugar

Skin the tomatoes and cut them up. Place in a strong pan with the grated orange rind, juice of the oranges and lemon and sugar. Boil gently, stirring from time to time for about 1 hour. Test for setting. When ready, pour into warmed jars and tie down when cold.

Cyril Curtis
From an old Somerset recipe book

RUNNER BEAN CHUTNEY (SWEET)

This is an excellent recipe and keeps well.

900 g (2 lb) runner beans, when
   trimmed and sliced
675 g (1½ lb) onions, when
   chopped
1 heaped tbsp cornflour
1 tbsp turmeric
1 heaped tbsp dry mustard
450 g (1 lb) demerara sugar
450 g (1 lb) brown sugar
850 ml (1½ pts) malt vinegar

Prepare vegetables. Cook sliced beans in well salted water until tender. Cook chopped onions in 300 ml (½ pt) of the vinegar.

Mix dry ingredients to a smooth paste with vinegar. Strain cooked beans, add remaining vinegar and cook for 10 minutes, add sugar and rest of ingredients and boil for a further 15 minutes, bottle and cover.

Albert Tucker
Chilcompton
Somerset

TOMATO CHUTNEY

Another very old recipe dating back to 1800.

450 g (1 lb) cooking apples, when peeled
450 g (1 lb) dates
450 g (1 lb) onions
675 g (1½ lb) red tomatoes, skinned
350 g (12 oz) sugar
850 ml (1½ pts) best malt vinegar
30 g (1 oz) cooking salt
15 g (½ oz) mustard seed

Chop apples, dates, and onions finely.

Skin tomatoes and add to ingredients.

Boil for 1¼ hours.

Leave to cool, then pot into jars and seal.

Evelyn Curtis
Lavenham

AUTUMN FRUIT CHUTNEY

If liked, for a less sweet chutney replace 450 g (1 lb) of apples with the same weight of chopped onions.
Makes about 8–9 jars

1.4 kg (3 lb) cooking apples
450 g (1 lb) pears
900 g (2 lb) tomatoes
450 g (1 lb) dates, chopped
900 g (2 lb) brown sugar
1 tsp each of cayenne pepper, salt, ground cinnamon and ginger
2 tsp mixed spice
600 ml (1 pt) malt vinegar

Skin, deseed and chop the tomatoes – you could use half green/half red.

Peel core and chop the apples and pears and put with the rest of the ingredients into a large pan and bring slowly to the boil.

Simmer gently until the fruit is tender and the chutney reaches the consistency of thick jam, with no water lying on top.

Pour into warm sterilised jars and cover when cold.

Celia Goodrick-Clarke
Cookery Writer, Daily Mail

MARROW AND APPLE CHUTNEY

675 g (1½ lb) diced marrow
225 g (½ lb) chopped onion
350 g (¾ lb) green apples
225 g (½ lb) brown sugar
850 ml (1½ pts) malt vinegar
15 g (½ oz) bruised whole ginger and peppercorns

Layer the diced marrow with salt in a basin and leave overnight. Drain off well, then add chopped

onion and apples and place in a pan with the other dry ingredients and spices tied in muslin.

Cook slowly until tender, then add the vinegar and proceed until a jam consistency is reached. Remove the spice bag and pot immediately.

Doreen Brinkley
Lavenham

MILITARY PICKLES

1 cauliflower
1 small marrow
450 g (1 lb) pickling onions
1 cucumber
1 tbsp mustard
1 tbsp flour
1 tbsp turmeric
115 g (¼ lb) sugar
1.2 ltrs (2 pts) malt vinegar

Peel and cut onions, wash, drain and cut cauliflower, cut up marrow and cucumber. Place vegetables in a pan. Sprinkle with salt. Leave for 24 hours. Then put vegetables, vinegar and sugar in a saucepan, bring to the boil.

Mix flour, turmeric and mustard into a smooth paste with a little vinegar, add to the vegetables when boiling.

Boil for 10 minutes, stirring all the time. Bottle in warm jars. Do not cover until cold.

Norah Eyles
Chilcompton
Somerset

IMPERIAL/METRIC EQUIVALENTS

Many people get confused with metric measurements. This isn't surprising when you think that one ounce is equivalent to 28.5 grammes and one fluid ounce converts to 28.5 millilitres. To try and make things slightly easier I have rounded all the metric measurements up or down to the nearest 5 grammes or 5 millilitres, but in some cases I have used The Guild of Food Writers' metrication chart, which I use for reference. Basically the Guild takes a gram-friendly policy – taking convenient metric weights and giving the UK equivalent in a less user-friendly amount. Either way you can't go wrong as I have given the UK Imperial measurements in all the recipes.

WEIGHT

The Imperial pound (lb) approximately equals 450 g—slightly less than ½ kilogram (500 g).

Imperial	Approx. metric equivalent
1 oz	25 g
2 oz	50 g
3 oz	75 g
4 oz	100–125 g
5 oz	150 g
6 oz	175 g
7 oz	200 g
8 oz	225 g
9 oz	250 g
10 oz	275 g
11 oz	300 g
12 oz	325–350 g
13 oz	375 g
14 oz	400 g
15 oz	425 g
16 oz (1 lb)	450 g
1½ lb	700 g

LIQUID CAPACITY

The Imperial pint (20 fluid oz) measures slightly more than ½ litre—approximately 575 millilitres (ml).

Imperial	Approx. metric equivalent
1 fluid oz	25 ml
2 fluid oz	50 ml
3 fluid oz	75 ml
4 fluid oz	100–125ml
5 fluid oz	150 ml
6 fluid oz	175 ml
7 fluid oz	200 ml
8 fluid oz	225 ml
9 fluid oz	250 ml
10 fluid oz (½ pint)	275–300 ml
20 fluid oz (1 pint)	575–600 ml

OVEN TEMPERATURES

The thermostatic dials on some electric cookers are marked in Centigrade. These correspond to Fahrenheit and gas markings as follows:

°F	°C	Gas mark	Temperature
250	130	½	Very cool
275	140	1	Very cool
300	150	2	Cool
325	160 / 170	3	Warm
350	180	4	Moderate
375	190	5	Fairly hot
400	200	6	Fairly hot
425	210 / 220	7	Hot
450	230	8	Very hot
475	240	9	Very hot

AMERICAN MEASURES

1 pint	= 16 fluid oz	= 453 cc
1 cup	= 8 fluid oz	= 227 cc
½ cup	= 4 tablespoonfuls of fluid	
1 cup butter	= 5 oz	= 142 gms
1 cup grated cheese	= 3½ oz	= 98 gms
1 cup sugar	= 7½ oz	= 223 gms
1 cup flour	= 4½ oz	= 128 gms

GELATINE

1 oz gelatine will stiffen 1 pint fluid or fruit juice; ½ oz gelatine will stiffen 1 pint mayonnaise or thick sauce

HINTS AND TIPS

AROUND THE HOUSE

■ A paperclip by the central fold will prevent a newspaper falling apart.

■ If your zip fastener does not run freely, rub the teeth with a lead pencil.

■ Place a small button at the end of your sellotape roll – the roll will be easier to find and the button easily removed.

■ To loosen sellotape that has become stuck, heat over steam for a couple of seconds and it will come away immediately.

■ Rub furniture polish on a metal curtain track to prevent rust and promote smooth running.

■ Talcum powder applied to curtain rails assists drawing and opening curtains, particularly if the rails are slightly rusty.

■ Window cleaning: Alternative aids are: 1) A little vinegar in plain warm water. 2) Methylated spirits. 3) Old newspaper crumpled into a ball and slightly damped. This is both effective and economical. Polish off with dry newspaper.

MAKE-UP TIPS

■ To soothe tired eyes, put pads of cotton wool in a jar and cover with witch hazel. Leave in the fridge until needed. Place one pad on each eye and relax. Thin slices of cucumber may also be used.

■ To strengthen nails, soak fingertips in a cup of warm water containing a tablespoon of bicarbonate of soda. Dry and apply almond oil or handcream.

■ To help dandruff, mix equal parts vinegar and water, part hair all over and apply mixture to scalp with cotton wool. Use BEFORE shampooing.

■ A pleasant skin tonic is made up of 25 g (1 oz) liquid honey and 250 g (9 oz) of witch hazel or rose water. Mix well and use after cleansing. It refreshes the skin and prepares it for make-up and moisturiser.

■ For dry hair: a trace of handcream (not lotion) rubbed on the palms of the hands and then lightly smoothed over the hair before brushing helps to counteract dryness and controls fly-away ends.

IN THE KITCHEN

■ To clean the insides of silver teapots or jugs, put a tablespoon of washing soda and a few silver milk bottle tops in the teapot. Fill with boiling water and leave to stand. Rinse out well, leave to drain and dry thoroughly.

■ Add one teaspoon of mustard powder to the washing-up water to get the smell of fish off silver, and add one teaspoon of vinegar to remove it from china.

■ Soak egg spoons in the water in which the eggs have been boiled in order to remove egg stains.

■ If you have a stained saucepan, cook rhubarb or apple peel in it and the stains will disappear.

■ A slice of bread in a cake tin will keep the cake moist. When the bread dries out replace with a fresh slice.

■ To keep biscuits crisp, put a cube of sugar into the tin with them.

CHEFS' TIPS

■ Try cooking kippers in a tall jug of boiling water. Place them into the water head first, leave for above 5 minutes, remove from jug by their tails. You will have lovely cooked moist kippers and no fishy smells.

■ To prevent the smell of cooking cabbage or cauliflower, squeeze a little lemon juice into the water.

■ A tablespoon of vinegar added to a beef stew will make the meat more tender, as well as making it taste good.

■ Add a small quantity of vinegar to the water when boiling eggs to prevent the white from leaking out.

■ New potatoes that have been scraped can be kept without discolouration for several hours if they are covered in water to which a few tablespoons of milk have been added.

■ Dust scales with flour first when weighing treacle and it will flow off easily.

■ A small quantity of glycerine added to royal icing prevents it becoming too brittle.

■ To stop toast going soggy, tap each slice all over before putting in toast rack. This is known as 'kringling'.

■ Left over white wine which has gone bitter may be added to vinegar.

■ A tablespoon of prune juice added to soups etc. will enrich them.

■ When egg yolks are not wanted for immediate use, drop them into a basin of cold water and put them in a cool place; they will keep for days.

THE LIST IS ENDLESS!

GLOSSARY OF COOKING TERMS

Acidulated water Water to which lemon juice or vinegar has been added in which fruit or vegetables, such as pears or Jerusalem artichokes, are immersed to prevent discolouration.

Agar-agar Obtained from various types of seaweed, this is a useful vegetarian alternative to gelatine.

Al dente Italian term used to describe food, especially pasta and vegetables, which are cooked until tender but still firm to the bite.

Arrowroot Fine, white powder used as a thickening agent for sauces. Unlike cornflour, it gives a clear gloss.

Au gratin Describes a dish which has been coated with sauce, then sprinkled with breadcrumbs or cheese and browned under the grill or in the oven.

Bain-marie Literally, a water bath, used to keep foods, such as delicate custards and sauces, at a constant low temperature during cooking. On the hob a double saucepan or bowl over a pan of simmering water is used: for oven cooking, the baking dish(es) is placed in a roasting tin containing sufficient hot water to come halfway up the sides.

Baking blind Pre-baking a pastry case before filling. Pastry case is lined with greaseproof paper and weighted down with dried beans or ceramic baking beans.

Baking powder A raising agent consisting of an acid, usually cream of tartar and an alkali, such as bicarbonate of soda. This expands during baking making cakes and breads rise.

Balsamic vinegar Italian oak-aged vinegar, dark brown in colour and has superior sweet, mellow flavour.

Bard To cover breast of game birds or poultry, or lean meat with fat to prevent the meat from drying out during roasting.

Baste To spoon juices and melted fat over meat, poultry, game or vegetables during roasting to keep them moist.

Béchamel Classic French white sauce, used as basis for other sauces and savoury dishes.

Beurre manié Equal parts of flour and butter kneaded together to form a paste. Used for thickening soups, stews and casseroles. Whisked into the hot liquid a little at a time at the end of cooking.

Blanch To immerse food briefly in fast-boiling water loosens skins, such as peaches or tomatoes – removes bitterness, destroys enzymes and preserves the colour, flavour and texture of vegetables (especially prior to freezing).

Bouquet garni Small bunch of herbs – a mixture of parsley stems, thyme and a bay leaf – tied in muslin – used to flavour stocks, soups and stews.

Braise To cook meat, poultry, game or vegetables slowly in a small amount of liquid in pan or casserole with a tight-fitting lid. Food is usually first browned in oil or fat.

Brochette Food cooked on a skewer or spit.

Brûlée A French term, meaning 'burnt' and used to refer to a dish with a crisp coating of caramelised sugar.

Canapé Small appetiser, consisting of a pastry or bread base with savoury topping, served with drinks.

Candying Preserving fruit or peel by impregnating with sugar.

Caper Small bud of a Mediterranean flowering shrub, packed in brine. Small French capers in balsamic vinegar – considered to be the best.

Caramelise Heat sugar or sugar syrup slowly until it is brown in colour; forms a caramel.

Carbonade Rich stews or braise of meat which includes beer.

Charcuterie French term for cooked pork, including hams, sausages and terrines.

Chine Sever the rib bones from the backbone, close to spine. This is done to meat joints, such as loin of pork or lamb, makes them easier to carve into chops after cooking.

Clarify Remove sediment or impurities from a liquid. Stock is clarified by heating with egg white – butter is clarified by melting and skimming. Butter which is clarified will withstand a higher frying temperature.
TO CLARIFY BUTTER heat until melted and bubbling stops. Remove from heat and let stand until sediment has sunk to the bottom – gently pour off the fat, straining through muslin.

Coconut milk Used in curries and other ethnic dishes. Available in cans from larger supermarkets and ethnic stores. Alternatively, creamed coconut sold compressed in blocks, can be reconstituted to make coconut milk.

Compote Mixture of fresh or dried fruit stewed in sugar syrup. Can be served hot or cold.

Concassé Diced fresh ingredient, used as a garnish – the term is most often applied to skinned, seeded tomatoes.

Coulis A smooth fruit or vegetable purée, thinned if necessary to a pouring consistency.

Court bouillon Aromatic cooking liquid containing wine, vinegar or lemon juice, used for poaching delicate fish, poultry or vegetables.

Cream of tartar Also known as tartaric acid, this is a raising agent which is also an ingredient of baking powder and self-raising flour.

Crêpe French term for a pancake.

Crimp To decorate the edge of pie, tart, or shortbread by pinching it at regular intervals – gives a fluted effect.

Croquette Seasoned mixture of cooked potato, fish, meat and poultry, or vegetables, shaped into small rolls, coated with egg and breadcrumbs and shallow-fried.

Croûte Circle or other shaped piece of fried bread, used as a base for serving small game birds.

Croûtons Small pieces of fried or toasted bread, served with soups and salads.

Crudités Raw vegetables, cut into slices or sticks, served with a dipping sauce as an appetiser.

Crystallise Preserve fruit in sugar syrup.

Curds Part of milk which coagulates when natural fermentation takes place or when a curdling agent, such as rennet, is added.

Cure To preserve fish, meat or poultry by smoking, drying or salting.

Deglaze To heat stock, wine or other liquid with the cooking juices left in the pan after roasting or sautéing, scraping and stirring to dissolve the sediment on base of the pan.

Dégorge Draw out moisture from a food, eg salting aubergines to remove bitter juices.

Dredge Sprinkle food generously with flour, sugar, icing sugar etc.

Dust Sprinkle lightly with flour, cornflour, icing sugar.

Emulsion A mixture of two liquids which do not dissolve into one another – oil and vinegar. Vigorous shaking or heating will emulsify them, as for a vinaigrette.

En croûte Food which is wrapped in pastry before cooking.

En papillote Food which is baked in a greaseproof paper or baking parchment parcel and served from the paper.

Escalope Thin slice of meat, such as pork, veal or turkey, cut from the top of the leg and pan-fried.

Extract Concentrated flavouring used in small quantities, eg yeast extract, vanilla extract.

Farce Another term for stuffing.

Fillet Term used to describe boned breasts of birds, boned sides of fish, the undercut of a loin of beef, lamb, port or veal etc.

Filo Pastry Type of Greek pastry manufactured in wafer-thin sheets and sold in packets or boxes. Must be kept covered to prevent it drying out.

Fine herbes French mixture of chopped herbs, ie parsley, tarragon, chives and chervil.

Flambé Flavouring a dish with alcohol – brandy or rum, which is then ignited so that the actual alcohol content is burned off.

Frosting Coat leaves and flowers with a fine layer of sugar to use as a decoration. An American term for icing cakes.

Galette A cooked savoury or sweet mixture shaped into a round.

Garnish Decoration, usually edible, such as parsley or lemon, which is used to enhance the appearance of a savoury dish.

Gelatine An animal-derived gelling agent sold in powdered form, and as leaf gelatine. Used in jellies, mousses and cold soufflés.

Gelazone A vegetarian gelling agent sold in powdered form in sachets – used as a substitute for gelatine.

Ghee Clarified butter widely used in Indian cookery.

Glaze Glossy coating given to sweet and savoury dishes – improves their appearance and sometimes flavour. Ingredients for glazes include beaten egg, egg white, milk and syrup.

Gluten Protein constituent of grains, such as wheat and rye, which develops when the flour is mixed with water to give the dough elasticity.

Griddle Flat, heavy, metal plate used on the hob for cooking scones or for searing savoury ingredients.

Hors d'oeuvre Selection of cold foods served together as an appetiser.

Hull To remove the stalk and calyx from soft fruits, such as strawberries etc.

Infuse Immerse flavourings, such as aromatic vegetables, herbs, spices and vanilla, in a liquid to impart flavour. The infused liquid is brought to the boil, then left to stand for a while.

Julienne Fine 'matchstick' strips of vegetables or citrus zest, used as a garnish.

Knead To work dough by pummelling with the heel of the hand.

Knock back Knead a yeast dough for a second time after rising, to ensure an even texture.

Liaison Thickening or binding agent based on a combination of ingredients, such as flour and water, or oil and egg.

Macerate Soften and flavour raw or dried foods by soaking in a liquid, eg soaking fruit in alcohol.

Mandolin(e) Flat wooden, or metal frame with adjustable cutting blades for cutting vegetables.

Marinate To soak raw meat, poultry or game – in a mixture of oil, wine, vinegar and flavourings – to soften and impart flavour. The mixture, which is known as a marinade, can also be used to baste the food during cooking.

Medallion Small round piece of meat – beef or veal.

Mocha Term means a blend of chocolate and coffee.

Parboil Boil a vegetable or other food for part of its cooking time before finishing it by another method.

Pare Finely peel the skin or zest from vegetables or fruit.

Passata A purée of plum tomatoes, used in many Italian dishes. Ready-made from supermarkets.

Pâte French word for pastry, familiar in pâte sucrée, a sweet flan pastry.

Pâté Savoury mixture of finely chopped or minced meat, fish and/or vegetables, served as a starter with bread or toast and crudités.

Pectin A naturally occurring substance found in most varieties of fruit and some vegetables – necessary for setting jams and jellies. Commercial pectin and sugar with pectin are also available for preserve-making.

Pesto Paste-like sauce made from puréed herbs and oil, used to flavour pasta and vegetables. A classic pesto is made from basil, pine nuts, garlic and olive oil.

Pickle Preserve meat or vegetables in brine or vinegar.

Poach Cook food gently in liquid at simmering point, so that the surface of the liquid is just trembling.

Pot roast Cook meat in a covered pan with some fat and a little liquid.

Prove Leave bread dough to rise after shaping.

Purée Pound, sieve or liquidise fruit, vegetables or fish to a smooth pulp. Purées often form the basis for soups and sauces.

Quenelles Fish, meat or poultry blended to a fine paste and shaped into ovals, then poached in a liquid.

Reduce Fast-boil stock or other liquid in an uncovered pan to evaporate water and concentrate the flavour.

Refresh To cool hot vegetables quickly by plunging into ice-cold water or holding under running water – stops the cooking process and preserves the colour.

Render Melt fat slowly to a liquid, either by heating meat trimmings, or to release the fat from fatty meat, ie duck or goose, during roasting.

Rennet Animal-derived enzyme used to coagulate milk in cheese-making. Vegetarian alternative is available.

Roulade Soufflé or sponge mixture usually rolled around a savoury or sweet filling.

Roux Mixture of equal quantities of butter (or other fat) and flour cooked together to form the basis of many sauces.

Salsa Piquant sauce made from chopped fresh vegetables and fruit.

Sauté Cook food in a small quantity of fat over a high heat, shaking the pan constantly – in a sauté pan (a frying pan with straight sides and a wide base).

Scald Pour boiling water over food to clean it, or loosen skin, eg tomatoes. Also used to describe heating milk to just below boiling point.

Score Cut parallel lines in the surface of food to improve its appearance or help it cook more quickly.

Sear Brown meat quickly in a little hot fat before grilling or roasting.

Shred Grate cheese or slice vegetables into very fine pieces or strips.

Sieve Press food through a perforated sieve to obtain a smooth texture.

Simmer Keep a liquid just below boiling point.

Skim Remove froth, scum or fat from the surface of stock, gravy, stews, jam etc. Use a skimmer, a spoon or absorbent kitchen paper.

Smoke Cure meat, poultry and fish by exposure to wood smoke.

Spit Rotating rod on which meat, poultry or game is cooked – in an oven or over an open fire.

Souse Pickle food, fish etc. in vinegar flavoured with spices.

Steep Immerse food in warm or cold liquid to soften it, and sometimes to draw out strong flavours.

Sterilise Destroy bacteria in foods by heating.

Stew Cook food, such as tougher cuts of meat, slowly in flavoured liquid which is kept at simmering point.

Stir-fry To cook small even-sized pieces of food rapidly in a little fat, tossing constantly over a high heat, usually in a wok.

Sweat Cook chopped or sliced vegetables in a little fat without liquid in covered pan over a low heat.

Syrup, sugar Concentrated solution of sugar in water used to make sorbets, granitas, fruit juices etc.

Tepid Term used to describe temperature at approximately blood heat, ie 37°C (98.7°F).

Thermometer, Sugar/Fat Used for accurately checking temperature of boiling sugar syrups, and fat for deep-frying, respectively.

Unleavened Bread made without a raising agent.

Vanilla sugar Sugar in which a vanilla pod has been stored to impart its flavour.

Zest Thin coloured outer layer of citrus fruit which contains essential oil.

Zester Small bevelled tool with five holes drawn across citrus fruit to remove the zest in fine strips.

SEASONS – FRUITS AND VEGETABLES

WHEN *FRUITS* ARE IN SEASON

This is to show when British-grown fruit is available.

	Jan	Feb	Mar	Apr	May	June	July	Aug	Sept	Oct	Nov	Dec
Apples –												
Cooking	•	•	•	•	•	•			•	•	•	•
Dessert	•	•	•							•	•	•
Blackberries									•	•		
Black/redcurrants						•	•	•				
Crab apples									•	•		
Cherries						•	•	•				
Chestnuts										•	•	•
Damsons								•	•	•		
Elderberries									•	•		
Gooseberries						•	•	•				
Greengages							•	•				
Loganberries							•	•				
Medlars										•	•	
Mulberries							•	•				
Pears	•	•	•					•	•	•	•	•
Plums						•	•	•	•	•		
Quinces										•	•	
Raspberries						•	•	•	•			
Rhubarb			•	•	•	•						
Strawberries					•	•	•	•	•	•		

WHEN *VEGETABLES* ARE IN SEASON

This is to show when British-grown vegetables are available.

	Jan	Feb	Mar	Apr	May	June	July	Aug	Sept	Oct	Nov	Dec
Artichokes –												
Globe						•	•	•	•			
Jerusalem	•	•	•	•						•	•	•
Asparagus					•	•						
Beans –												
Broad						•	•					
Runner							•	•	•	•		
Kidney						•	•	•	•			
Beetroot	•	•	•	•	•	•	•	•	•	•	•	•
Broccoli –												
Calabrese						•	•	•	•	•		
Sprouting			•	•	•							
Brussels –												
Top	•									•	•	•
Sprouts	•	•	•	•						•	•	•
Cabbage –												
January King	•	•	•	•						•	•	
Drum Head								•	•	•	•	
Spring Green	•	•	•								•	
Red	•	•										•
Carrot	•	•	•	•	•	•	•	•	•	•	•	•
Cauliflower	•	•	•	•	•	•	•	•	•	•	•	•
Celeriac	•	•	•						•	•		•
Celery				•	•	•	•	•	•	•	•	•
Chicory	•	•							•	•	•	•
Chinese Leaves				•	•	•	•	•	•	•	•	
Courgettes						•	•	•	•	•		
Cucumbers			•	•	•	•	•	•	•	•		
Endive				•	•	•	•					
Kale	•	•	•	•	•						•	•

WHEN *VEGETABLES* ARE IN SEASON

This is to show when British-grown vegetables are available.

	Jan	Feb	Mar	Apr	May	June	July	Aug	Sept	Oct	Nov	Dec
Leeks	•	•	•	•				•	•	•	•	•
Lettuce	•	•	•	•	•	•	•	•	•	•	•	•
Marrows						•	•	•	•	•		
Mint					•	•	•	•	•	•		
Mushrooms	•	•	•	•	•	•	•	•	•	•	•	•
Mustard and Cress	•	•	•	•	•	•	•	•	•	•		•
Onions	•								•	•		•
Parsley					•	•	•	•	•	•		
Parsnips	•	•	•	•					•	•	•	•
Peppers						•	•	•	•	•		
Peas						•	•	•	•	•		
Potatoes – New						•	•	•				
Potatoes – Maincrop	•	•	•	•	•				•	•		•
Pumpkin								•	•	•		
Radishes					•	•	•	•	•	•		
Seakale	•	•	•									•
Shallots	•								•	•	•	•
Spinach (best Mar/Apr)			•	•	•	•	•	•	•	•		
Spring onions				•	•	•	•	•				
Swedes	•	•	•	•	•				•	•	•	•
Sweetcorn								•	•	•		
Tomatoes					•	•	•	•	•	•		
Turnips	•	•	•			•	•	•	•	•	•	•
Watercress	•	•	•	•	•	•	•	•	•	•	•	•